Retire Early
Sleep Well

A practical guide to
modern portfolio theory
and retirement
in plain english.

Steven R. Davis

Boomer, retired at age 53

Copyright © 2002, Steven R. Davis.
All rights reserved.
Except as permitted under the United States Copyright Act of 1976,
no part of this publication may be reproduced or distributed in any form
or by any means, or stored in a database or retrieval system,
without the prior written permission of the publisher.

Retire Early Sleep Well
A practical guide to modern portfolio theory
and retirement in plain english

Steven R. Davis

ISBN: 0-9663436-4-6

Published by
Grote Publishing
2364 Jackson Street, #306
Stoughton, WI 53589
(608) 877-0766

Cover design by
Cox & Co.
Black Earth, WI
(608) 767-2181

Printed and bound by
Thomson-Shore, Inc., Dexter, MI.
Printed in the United States of America.

10 9 8 7 6 5 4 3 2

This publication is designed to provide accurate and authoritative information
in regard to the subject matter covered. It is sold with the understanding
that neither the author nor the publisher is engaged in rendering legal, accounting,
or other professional service. If legal advice or other expert professional assistance
is required, the services of a competent professional person should be sought.

From the Declaration of Principles
jointly adopted by a Committee of the American Bar Association
and a Committee of Publishers

Table of Contents

page

Introduction 5

Part 1 – Retirement Savings and Lifestyle Overhead
1 Caution – Retirement Ahead 9
2 The Power of Compounding 10
3 IRA's and 401(k)'s (the power of tax-deferred compounding) 11
4 Budgeting for Retirement 13
5 Sources of Retirement Income 14
6 Nestegg Rules of Thumb 15
7 Lifestyle Overhead 22
8 Saving 24

Part 2 – Investment Basics
9 Capitalism and Free Enterprise, the Engines of Wealth Creation 27
10 Active Management, The Loser's Game in an Efficient Market 28
11 Actual Mutual Fund Performance and Persistence of Performance
   (good past performance does not persist into the future) 31
12 Mutual Fund Operating Expenses 33
13 Turnover and Trading Costs 34
14 The Index Fund Advantage 36
15 Distributions and Taxes 38
16 Actual Results of Individuals (much poorer than you think) 39
17 Wall Street Misinformation, Technical and Fundamental Analysis ... 41

Part 3 – Modern Investing
18 Modern Portfolio Theory 45
19 Investment Statistics Basics 46
20 The Benefits of Low Correlation 48
21 Investment Risk Basics 50
22 Investment Return Basics 51
23 Asset Class Research 53
24 Small Cap and Value Stock Investing, The Three Factor Model 56
25 Fixed Income Investing 58
26 International Investing 59
27 Real Estate Asset Class Investing 60

Part 4 – Modern Portfolio Management
28 Asset Allocation 63
29 The Modern Power Portfolio 65
30 The Do-it-yourself Modern Portfolio 67
31 The Simplified Modern Portfolio 69
32 Making the Most of Your Plan's Funds 71
33 Working with a Financial Advisor 72
34 Rebalancing 73
35 Investment Policy 74

Part 5 – Retirement

36 Retirement Calculators and Withdrawal Strategies 77
37 Three Sleep Well Withdrawal Strategies 79
38 Boomers and Social Security; will it be there for us? 80
39 Social Security Benefits 82
40 Health Insurance in Early Retirement, Before Medicare Eligibility 85
41 Medicare, Medigap and Long Term Care Insurance 88
42 Retirement Lifestyle 91

Appendices

Appendix A The Timeline of Risk Management Breakthroughs 95
Appendix B Reading List and Web Sites 97
Appendix C Power of Compounding and Lifestyle Overhead Examples 99
Appendix D Glossary 109

Introduction

How can we be assured of reasonable returns and avoid catastrophic losses in the market? How much do I need to retire? I wrote this book to save you the trouble of sorting through all the conflicting information out there to develop answers to these simple questions about investing and retirement.

This is a short book, with very short chapters, because the information you need to plan and invest for retirement is really fairly simple. If you want to read a lot, check out the references and the suggested reading list (they will allow you to dig into areas of interest as deeply as you wish).

I've distilled each chapter into an "abstract" at the top of the chapter. I suggest that you start by reading all of the "abstracts" straight through from the beginning. This will provide you with a good introduction to the material as a whole, and provide a helpful context as you read each chapter in detail.

In addition I have provided "navigation tips" at various points to help you navigate to topics of interest (sometimes skipping over sections of the book, sometimes skipping part of a chapter).

A Glossary is included at the end to help you with unfamiliar investment terminology.

Most Americans are living beyond their means and for that reason will not be able to retire in comfort. The average among us are spending every dime they get – and then some. The more affluent are eating out, buying luxury cars and "starter castles." Most are nearly oblivious of the need to save aggressively to provide the possibility of comfortable retirement.

We are faced with a whole generation that has failed to save adequately for retirement, and then in effect "gambling" what nesteggs they have on questionable advice from Wall Street or more personal "crap shoots." We are led to believe that beating the market is a matter of getting the right advice. But research indicates that both professional and individual investors, on average, fail to achieve market returns; and individual investors fail miserably.

Most of the investment advice available from Wall Street and the financial media ignores the developments of modern portfolio theory over the last 50 years. The industry that we turn to for advice about stock picking, market timing and mutual fund picking is very slow to inform us that the overwhelming body of research has discredited their active management strategies.

I am not an investment advisor. I am not even an accountant. I'm an architect, but I know the kind of information I needed (and had to work so hard to find and assemble). I'm writing this book because it just doesn't have to be that hard and because my notes, and outlines of materials were so helpful and useful to friends and associates. They all wanted **a single** book to read, and while many books, particularly the ones on the suggested reading list, are quite good (on some part or even many parts of the subject) not one of them was simple and complete enough for me to recommend alone.

Most of the books about modern portfolio theory are not written in "plain english" and most of the books on retirement planning ignore modern portfolio theory. Retirement planning without modern portfolio theory is dangerous to your wealth.

I eventually satisfied myself that I had answered all my questions and had prepared well for retirement. On August 1, 2001, I retired (at the age of 53). I have been involved in the executive management (and ownership) of large design and construction firms since I was 35 years old. I am a middle-aged boomer who is looking forward to many years of retirement. My wife and I are not wealthy, though we are comfortable. We are not overly worried about the future. Our nestegg is invested well and we sleep well.

What follows is an easy to read, "plain english" guide to investing and retirement based on the Nobel Prize winning strategies of Modern Portfolio Theory and the thrift and sensible savings ethic that made America great.

I hope that you too can **Retire Early Sleep Well**.

Part One

Retirement Savings and Lifestyle Overhead

Chapter 1
Caution - Retirement Ahead

> Abstract – The median Net Worth of Households (especially of Boomers approaching retirement) is far too low to provide significant income in retirement.

Retirement is a relatively new concept. Until the last half of the twentieth century retirement was not common. When social security was enacted in 1935, benefits started later than the average life expectancy. Retirement at first was a handful of golden years to be enjoyed in peace, by a small minority of seniors, at the end of a long life of hard work. The idea of 20 or 30 years of retirement is only beginning to be comprehended.

As the baby boomers grow older, the first of them are reaching the age of early retirement. Only those who have built significant nesteggs will be able to retire at around 55 years of age and forgo the last 10 years of the now typical working life. Most of the rest of the boomers will not even be able to retire in comfort at age 65. Many will have to work to age 70 to retire in anything approaching comfort. Real comfort will not be possible for far too many, at any age. Too many are depending too much on Social Security and most have saved far too little, or have no nestegg at all.

> *"There is broad general agreement that America is about to launch an entire generation into retirement without sufficient financial resources to support them. These retirees can expect to live longer, retire earlier, and endure inflation longer than any generation that preceded them. ... There is also broad general agreement that America has one of the lowest savings rates in the world."*
>
> Frank Armstrong, Investment Strategies for the 21st Century

The savings rates of most of those approaching retirement are probably inadequate. The total net worth of families in America according to the Federal Reserve Survey of Consumer Finances reveals that net worths are generally far lower than can be expected to support retirement. The net worth of households in America as of 1998 is shown in Table 1.1 (many have lost ground since then in the down markets). The 2001 survey will be published in early 2003.

TABLE 1.1 NET WORTH OF HOUSEHOLDS IN AMERICA IN 1998 (US Dollars)

age	Median	top 25%	top 10%	top 5%	top 1%
20 to 29 yrs	$5,200	$25,400	$78,300	$148,200	$383,300
30 to 39	34,700	127,400	267,500	451,100	1,210,100
40 to 49	86,200	226,800	531,600	829,000	3,402,000
50 to 59	120,900	326,700	708,800	1,410,600	5,791,700
60 to 69	155,800	356,700	902,800	1,850,200	6,263,400
70 to 79	140,900	316,500	703,400	1,074,500	4,338,100
80 and over	118,000	252,200	440,000	693,000	2,057,800

The 50 to 59 year olds approaching retirement have a median net worth of only $120,900, and about half of that is tied up in their houses. That means they have only about $60,000 in their retirement nesteggs. In fact, much of the net worth of families with net worths under $500,000 is tied up in their houses. The retirement nesteggs of most families approaching retirement is far too small to allow comfortable retirement.

How is your nestegg doing? How can you accumulate $500,000 or $1,000,000 or more? The answer is a little at a time with the power of compounding.

Chapter 2
The Power of Compounding

> Abstract - Start early; the power of compounding takes time, but is very powerful. If you wait 10 years to get started, you will have about 1/3 as much at retirement.

Albert Einstein thought that one of his most important contributions was the Rule of 72 (which he is credited with discovering) involving the **power of compounding**. The rule of 72 states that the number of years to double your money at a given return is 72 divided by the rate of return (e.g. 72 divided by 10% = 7.2 years). Compounding is the power at work in the children's object lesson that involves the value of doubling a penny every day for a month. Most are astounded to find that the final value is over $5,000,000 (See Appendix C).

Similarly, the growth of a nestegg's value is deceptively slow in the beginning – but almost spectacular in the out years – underlining the importance of beginning early in investing for retirement. In the table below you can see how the annual investment of $1,000 each year would grow over 40 years (at 10% return).

TABLE 2.1 40 YEAR COMPOUNDED GROWTH OF $1,000

Annual Investment		10 years	20 years	30 years	40 years
$1,000	with no taxes	17,531	63,002	180,943	486,852

Notice particularly what happens in the out years, between 20 and 40 years, the growth of the investment is quite dramatic; and obviously not mainly from the new money invested each year. Most of the growth is coming from the power of compounding. You can also see how much less you will have if you wait another 10 years to get started with your retirement savings! If you wait 10 years to get started, you will have about 1/3 as much at retirement.

The picture changes dramatically when you introduce the drag of annual taxes on a taxable account. The next table outlines investments of from $1,000 to $10,000 per year in both taxable and tax-deferred accounts (See Appendix C for details of these examples).

TABLE 2.2 40 YEAR TAXABLE AND TAX-DEFERRED INVESTMENT PRO-FORMA
Assuming 10% return and 32% total taxes (federal, state and local combined)

Annual Investment		10 years	20 years	30 years	40 years
$1,000	Tax-deferred (IRA)	17,531	63,002	180,943	486,852
	Taxable	14,617	42,839	97,326	202,523
$3,000	Tax-deferred (IRA)	52,594	189,007	542,830	1,460,555
	Taxable	43,852	128,516	291,977	607,569
$5,000	Tax-deferred (IRA)	87,656	315,012	904,717	2,434,259
	Taxable	73,087	214,194	486,629	1,012,616
$10,000	Tax-deferred (IRA)	175,312	630,025	1,809,434	4,868,518
	Taxable	146,173	428,388	973,257	2,025,231

The lesson: **invest as much as you can in tax-deferred accounts.**

The next chapter outlines your tax-deferred alternatives.

Chapter 3
IRA's and 401(k)'s
(the power of tax-deferred compounding)

> Abstract – Maximize your contributions to all available tax-deferred accounts.
> Always contribute to any level matched by your employer.

Everyone should have an IRA, a 401(k) or some other of the many forms of tax-deferred savings and retirement plans allowed by the federal government. They provide a **very** significant advantage over taxable investments.

> **Navigation Tip**
> The rest of this chapter contains a lot of details about contribution amounts and rules. You can skip over it for now and come back to it when you need particular details later.

Individual Retirement Accounts (IRA's)

There are two main types of IRA's, the Traditional IRA and the Roth IRA. Contributions to both traditional and Roth IRA's are limited to amounts in the following table. If you are over 50 you can make an additional "catch-up" contribution.

TABLE 3.1 TRADITIONAL and ROTH IRA CONTRIBUTION LIMITS

	Maximum Contribution	Catch-up Contribution
2002 – 2004	$3,000	$500
2005	$4,000	$500
2006 – 2007	$4,000	$1,000
2008	$5,000	$1,000
2009 on	indexed with inflation in $500 increments	

IRA investments cannot be withdrawn before age 59½ (withdrawal before then will cost you a 10% Federal penalty). Roth IRA's are taxed differently from traditional IRA's. Traditional IRA's have deductible contributions and taxable withdrawals. Roth IRA's have non-deductible contributions and tax-free withdrawals.

Traditional IRA's. You must start taking Required Minimum Distributions from a traditional IRA by age 70½. Withdrawals are taxed as personal income. If you participate in a 401(k), or other qualified plan, you can still contribute to a traditional IRA. But your contribution will be fully deductible only if your Modified Adjusted Gross Income (MAGI) is less than $34,000 ($54,000 if married); and not deductible at all if your MAGI is over $44,000 ($64,000 if married). If you do not participate in a 401(k), but your spouse does, your traditional IRA contribution is fully deductible only if your MAGI is less than $150,000 (filing jointly); and not deductible at all if your MAGI is $160,000 (filing jointly).

Roth IRA's. There are no Required Minimum Distributions from a Roth IRA. You can contribute to a Roth IRA if your MAGI is less than $95,000 ($150,000 if married). Above $95,000 AGI ($150,000 if married) your allowable contribution is reduced on a sliding scale reaching zero at $110,000 AGI ($160,000 if married). You must contribute the full $3,000 (or the maximum allowable) to a Roth IRA. If you participate in a 401(k), or other qualified plan, you can still contribute to a Roth IRA.

Educational IRA's. Contributions to an educational IRA may be made for children under 18 years of age. Distributions can be used for elementary, secondary and higher education. The phase out range for individuals remains $95,000 to $110,000, but has been raised for joint filers to $190,000 to $220,000. The maximum contribution is $2,000 per year.

IRA's for Small Businesses and Self-employed Individuals

SIMPLE IRA's. Businesses with less than 100 employees (including self-employed individuals) can establish and contribute to SIMPLE IRA's. Both employer and employee can make contributions.

TABLE 3.2   **SIMPLE IRA CONTRIBUTION LIMITS**

Year	Maximum Contribution	Catch-up Contribution
2002	$7,000	$500
2003	$8,000	$1,000
2004	$9,000	$1,500
2005	$10,000	$2,000
2006	indexed with inflation in $500 increments	

SEP IRA's. Simplified Employees Pension (SEP) plans allow larger contributions, but can only be contributed to by the employer (including self-employed individuals). Catch-up contributions are allowed at the same levels as the 401k below.

TABLE 3.3   **SEP IRA CONTRIBUTION LIMITS**

Year	Maximum Employer Contribution	Maximum Self-employed Individual Contribution
2002	25% of compensation or $40,000 whichever is less	25% of earned income or $40,000 whichever is less

KEOGH (HR 10) PLANS. Keogh plans may be either defined contribution plans or defined benefit plans with generous contribution and benefit limits.

401(k) Plans

There are many forms of employer-provided plans including 401(k) and 403(b) plans. In 2002, an employee may contribute up to 25% of compensation or $11,000, whichever is less. Many employers match employee contributions (up to the some limit), or simply contribute to the plan in the employee's name. Maximum total is $40,000 or 100% of compensation whichever is less.

TABLE 3.3   **401(k) and 403(b) CONTRIBUTION LIMITS**

Year	Maximum Contribution	Catch-up Contribution
2002	$11,000	$1,000
2003	$12,000	$2,000
2004	$13,000	$3,000
2005	$14,000	$4,000
2006	$15,000	$5,000
2007 on	indexed with inflation in $500 increments	

You should **always** contribute to any level matched by your employer. Where else can you get a 100% (instant) investment return?

How much will you need to retire? How much will you need to save each year to accumulate that much by the time you want to retire? The next three chapters cover how to budget for retirement, the sources of income in retirement, and provide nestegg rules of thumb (how much you need to be saving for retirement).

Chapter 4
Budgeting for Retirement

Abstract - To plan for retirement you must first determine how much income you want in retirement. If you are between 20 and 40 years old, assume it will be close to 90% or 100% of what you are making now. If you are between 40 and 50, you can probably use 80% of your current income. If you are over 50, you may be able to use as little as 70% of your current income. Knowing (in detail) how much you are spending now will help.

How much should you plan on spending in retirement? Conventional wisdom suggests that we can expect to live comfortably on 80 percent of pre-retirement income, but many experts recommend 90 percent or 100 percent or even more. If you are between 20 and 40 years old, I suggest you use at least 90% of your current income as a place to start. If you are between 40 and 50, you can probably use 80% of your current income. If you are over 50, you may be able to use as little as 70% of your current income. But if you plan to be very active and travel a lot more in retirement, you could easily spend as much as you do now – or more!

These percentage-based rules of thumb are probably a good way to plan at a distance of 10 or 20 years from retirement. As you get closer to your actual retirement you should budget with a lot more care and accuracy. In order to accurately estimate your post-retirement expenses, you will need to know what you are spending now. There are a lot of good ways to budget and a lot of good software available to help you like Quicken or Microsoft Money. Once you select the budget categories you want to track, you will need at least 12 months of expenses, because all months are not created equal. I used the following categories:

Housing (mortgage, taxes, utilities, repairs and maintenance – or rent)
Food (groceries and dining out)
Miscellaneous (the general catch-all; this one gets big)
Automobiles (loans, gas, oil, maintenance and repairs)
Insurance (general liability, life, house, health – especially before age 65)
Medical Expenses (not covered by insurance)
Recreation (club dues, green fees, skiing, etc.)
Travel (air fare, lodging, etc.)
Charity (charitable contributions)
Kids (school, general support and bailouts)
Taxes (federal, state and local income & capital gains taxes)
Savings and Investment (before retirement)

Some of these budget items will not change much after retirement. Some will change dramatically. Savings and investment will fall to zero. Your taxes are likely to be lower (the combination of savings and taxes can add up to as much as a 25% reduction by themselves). Housing, food, automobiles, etc. won't change much (until your mortgage is gone). Expenses related to kids will fall, but don't count on anything like zero. Health insurance and medical costs will be very different (sometimes higher, sometimes lower). Travel and recreation can vary a lot, even from year to year (be careful if you hope to travel a lot – it can be very expensive).

Once you have some idea of your retirement budget, you can begin to explore where the money will come from in retirement.

Chapter 5
Sources of Income in Retirement

Abstract - Sources of income in retirement are limited. If you don't have a pension, you will likely be left with only Social Security and your personal retirement nestegg. Social Security alone will barely get you to the poverty threshhold. You need a nestegg!

Sources of income in retirement are limited, in general including only pensions, Social Security and your personal retirement nestegg.

Pensions. Pensions are defined benefit plans, generally provided by your employer (either government or private industry). A defined benefit plan provides a "defined benefit" amount each year, sometimes with an annual cost of living adjustment. Fewer and fewer will have defined benefit plans (pensions) in the future. If you have one, it will still probably not provide all the income you need in retirement, even with Social Security. These plans are relentlessly being replaced by defined contribution plans in private industry.

In a defined contribution plan only the employers annual "contribution" to your account is defined; whatever it adds up to in the end will become part of your personal retirement savings nestegg.

Social Security. Your Social Security benefit will vary dramatically depending on your earnings and when you retire. Social Security benefits are discussed in detail later in chapters 38 and 39. Social Security alone will provide you with the lifestyle of the poor and helpless.

Personal Retirement Nestegg. You need a personal retirement nestegg to provide any income you need in addition to your Social Security benefit. If you don't save for your retirement, you will be left with only Social Security (and any pension). If you don't already have some idea how much you will need in your nestegg, the following chapter will be a big help.

The table below illustrates retirement scenarios for five hypothetical workers with incomes varying from $32,000 to $250,000 per year. For the purpose of the example, I have assumed that each of the workers needs 90% of that income in retirement and has no pension. The Social Security benefits in this example are from Table 39.3 (for illustration, at age 62).

TABLE 5.1   REQUIRED INCOME FROM NESTEGG

	A	B	C	D	E
Current Earnings	$32,000	$50,000	$80,000	120,000	250,000
Retirement Budget %	90%	90%	90%	90%	90%
Retirement Budget	$28,800	$45,000	$72,000	$108,000	225,000
Pension	0	0	0	0	0
Social Security (at age 62)	10,260	13,320	15,000	15,000	15,000
Social Security (spouse)	5,130	6,660	7,500	7,500	7,500
Required Income from Nestegg (nestegg withdrawal amount)	13,410	25,020	49,500	85,500	202,500

The next chapter will show you how large a nestegg each of these workers needs.

Chapter 6
Nestegg Rules of Thumb

Abstract - The tables and worksheet in this chapter will allow you to determine how large your nestegg will need to be at retirement and how much you need to be saving each year to meet the goal.

Knowing your required income from your nestegg in today's dollars would be fine if you're going to retire next year. But what about retirement 10, 20 or 30 years into the future? How should you account for expected inflation in your planning?

Let's take the example with the five hypothetical workers a little further and assume that they are each 35 years old, have saved absolutely nothing to date, and want to retire when they are 62 in 27 years. We already have their retirement budgets and income from nestegg requirements from Table 5.1 above. To change these withdrawal amounts from current dollars to retirement year dollars we need to multiply by a factor to account for inflation. The inflation factor for 27 years in Table 6.1 below is 2.22 (if we assume 3% inflation).

The inflation factors in Table 6.1 provide the multiplier for $1.00 (in current value) between 1 and 40 years in the future for both 3% and 4% inflation. Most financial planners use between 3% and 4% for planning purposes. In our example I have used 3%.

TABLE 6.1 INFLATION FACTOR

Inflation	3%	4%		3%	4%		3%	4%		3%	4%
Year 1	1.03	1.04	year 11	1.38	1.54	year 21	1.86	2.28	year 31	2.50	3.37
2	1.06	1.08	12	1.43	1.60	22	1.92	2.37	32	2.58	3.51
3	1.09	1.12	13	1.47	1.67	23	1.97	2.46	33	2.65	3.65
4	1.13	1.17	14	1.51	1.73	24	2.03	2.56	34	2.73	3.79
5	1.16	1.22	15	1.56	1.80	25	2.09	2.67	35	2.81	3.95
6	1.19	1.27	16	1.60	1.87	26	2.16	2.77	36	2.90	4.10
7	1.23	1.32	17	1.65	1.95	27	2.22	2.88	37	2.99	4.27
8	1.27	1.37	18	1.70	2.03	28	2.29	3.00	38	3.07	4.44
9	1.30	1.42	19	1.75	2.11	29	2.36	3.12	39	3.17	4.62
10	1.34	1.48	20	1.81	2.19	30	2.43	3.24	40	3.26	4.80

The following summarizes the inflation adjusted income from nestegg for our five workers.

TABLE 6.2 INFLATION ADJUSTED INCOME FROM NESTEGG

	A	B	C	D	E
Retirement Budget	$28,800	$45,000	$72,000	$108,000	225,000
Required Income from Nestegg	13,410	25,020	49,500	85,500	202,500
Retirement year w/d fr nestegg	29,770	55,544	109,890	189,810	449,550
(current dollars times 2.22)					

Social Security benefits are adjusted each year to reflect inflation and therefore do not need to be adjusted for this simplified analysis. Your pension, if you have one, may or may not be indexed.

Knowing our hypothetical workers' required withdrawal amounts at retirement will allow us to determine how large each of their nesteggs must be at their retirement. The required future size of your nestegg can be roughly estimated by dividing the required withdrawal amount by a reasonable withdrawal rate (say 6%). Some would argue that 4% or 5% are safer, but you can be too careful; and there are ways to manage retirement withdrawals that should allow 6% if you are careful (and flexible) in retirement. Some even propose 7% or 8%, but I think they are too aggressive to sleep well. See Chapters 36 and 37 for a discussion of withdrawal rates.

I am inclined to plan on retirement lasting indefinitely rather than guessing some finite number of years. You simply cannot afford to outlive your money. Being old and broke is no fun! A 6% withdrawal rate can be sustained if you are flexible in retirement and have a modern portfolio; a 4% withdrawal rate can be sustained under almost any circumstances.

You can use this rule of thumb (Nestegg = Withdrawal Amount divided by the Withdrawal Rate) or you can multiply the required withdrawal amount by the factor in Table 6.3 below for each $1.00 of withdrawal (16.67 at 6% withdrawal). Or, for a general idea of nestegg size you can interpolate between the amounts in the table.

TABLE 6.3   REQUIRED NESTEGG BASED ON WITHDRAWAL PERCENTAGE

Desired Annual Withdrawal	Required Nestegg at **6%** Withdrawal	Required Nestegg at **5%** Withdrawal	Required Nestegg at **4%** Withdrawal
$1.00	$16.67	$20.00	$25.00
1,000	16,667	20,000	25,000
10,000	166,667	200,000	250,000
25,000	416,667	500,000	625,000
50,000	833,333	1,000,000	1,250,000
75,000	1,250,000	1,500,000	1,875,000
100,000	1,666,666	2,000,000	2,500,000

Continuing with our example we can determine how large a nestegg these five hypothetical workers will need when they retire by multiplying the required withdrawal amount by 16.67 (assuming a 6% withdrawal rate).

TABLE 6.4   REQUIRED NESTEGG AMOUNTS

	A	B	C	D	E
Retirement Budget	$28,800	$45,000	$72,000	$108,000	225,000
Required Income from Nestegg	13,410	25,020	49,500	85,500	202,500
Retirement year w/d from nestegg	29,770	55,544	109,890	189,810	449,550
Required Nestegg (infl adj w/d amount times 16.67)	496,269	925,925	1,831,866	3,164,133	7,494,000

Don't confuse your total net worth with your nestegg. If you have a total net worth of $300,000 and $150,000 of it is the equity in your house and cars, you have only a $150,000 retirement nestegg. Your nestegg is your investment portfolio that can be liquidated and spent. You can't spend your house and cars.

How much would each of our five workers need to be saving each year to accumulate that size nestegg in 27 years? Table 6.5 provides a simple divisor for you to use. The variables in the table are the years to retirement and the return rate. Table 6.5 provides the amount that will accrue in from 1 to 40 years from the investment of $1.00 each year at returns from 8% to 12%.

Historical returns from investment portfolios are discussed in detail later, for now let's just assume they can get 10% per year. For our example, $1.00 invested in each of 27 years will grow to $122.29 at 10% return on investment. The required nestegg divided by $122.29 yields the amount that must be invested each year to grow a nestegg that size (see Table 6.6).

TABLE 6.5 REQUIRED INVESTMENT AMOUNT DIVISOR
(GROWTH OF $1.00 INVESTED EACH YEAR TAX DEFERRED)

Total Return		8%	9%	10%	11%	12%
Year	1	1.08	1.09	1.10	1.11	1.12
	2	2.17	2.19	2.21	2.23	2.25
	3	3.34	3.39	3.43	3.48	3.52
	4	4.61	4.69	4.77	4.86	4.95
	5	5.98	6.11	6.25	6.39	6.54
	6	7.45	7.66	7.88	8.10	8.33
	7	9.05	9.35	9.66	9.99	10.33
	8	10.77	11.19	11.63	12.09	12.56
	9	12.64	13.20	13.79	14.42	15.07
	10	14.65	15.39	16.17	17.00	17.88
	11	16.82	17.77	18.79	19.87	21.03
	12	19.16	20.37	21.67	23.06	24.55
	13	21.70	23.21	24.84	26.60	28.5
	14	24.43	26.30	28.32	30.52	32.92
	15	27.39	29.66	32.15	34.88	37.87
	16	30.58	33.33	36.37	39.72	43.41
	17	34.02	37.33	41.00	45.09	49.62
	18	37.75	41.69	46.10	51.04	56.57
	19	41.77	46.44	51.72	57.66	64.36
	20	46.11	51.62	57.89	65.00	73.09
	21	50.80	57.27	64.68	73.15	82.86
	22	55.86	63.42	72.14	82.20	93.80
	23	61.33	70.13	80.36	92.24	106.05
	24	67.23	77.44	89.39	103.39	119.78
	25	73.61	85.41	99.33	115.76	135.16
	26	80.50	94.10	110.27	129.49	152.37
	27	87.94	103.57	122.29	144.74	171.66
	28	95.98	113.89	135.52	161.66	193.26
	29	104.66	125.14	150.07	180.44	217.45
	30	114.03	137.40	166.08	201.29	244.54
	31	124.15	150.77	183.69	224.43	274.89
	32	135.08	165.34	203.06	250.12	308.87
	33	146.89	181.22	224.36	278.63	346.94
	34	159.64	198.53	247.80	310.28	389.57
	35	173.41	217.40	273.58	345.41	437.32
	36	188.28	237.96	301.94	384.41	490.80
	37	204.35	260.38	333.13	427.69	550.69
	38	221.70	284.81	367.44	475.74	617.78
	39	240.43	311.45	405.19	529.07	692.91
	40	260.67	340.48	446.71	588.27	777.06

TABLE 6.6 REQUIRED ANNUAL INVESTMENT TO MEET NESTEGG GOAL

	A	B	C	D	E
Retirement Budget	$28,800	$45,000	$72,000	$108,000	225,000
Required Income from Nestegg	13,410	25,020	49,500	85,500	202,500
Retirement year w/d from nestegg	29,770	55,544	109,890	189,810	449,550
Required Nestegg	496,269	925,925	1,831,866	3,164,133	7,494,000
Required Annual Investment (Required Nestegg divided by 122.29)	4,058	7,572	14,980	25,874	61,281
Savings as a % of income	12.68%	15.14%	18.72%	21.56%	24.51%

Very few are saving that much. Those that don't may not reach their goals. They will either have to work longer than they hoped, or spend less in retirement than they hoped – or both! In short, most are living beyond their means. The worksheet on the following page will help find how much **YOU** need to be saving to meet your goals.

Personal Retirement Planning Worksheet

Years to Retirement

- A **Current Age** your age today
- B **Retirement Age** age you want to retire. 55, 62, 65 or 70 (are easiest to use)
- C **Years to retirement** the only years left to save, invest and grow a nestegg (B minus A)

Current Earnings and Desired Retirement Income

- D **Current Earnings** total of your earnings and your spouse's earnings today
  In current dollars (not adjusted for inflation)
- E **Desired Retirement Income** either from a percentage, say 80%, 90% or 100%
  of your current earnings or actual budget In current dollars

Sources of Retirement Income (other than your nestegg)

- F **Pension** (if any)
- G **Social Security Benefits** from your Social Security Statement or
  an estimate from Table 39.3 (no benefits can be received before age 62)
- H **Social Security Benefits** (spouse) A min of 50% of your benefits
  (no benefits can be received before age 62)
- I (non nestegg) **Retirement Income Sub Total** (sum of F+G+H)

Nestegg Income

- J **Income Needed from Nestegg** the income you need from your nestegg (E minus I)
  In current dollars (not adjusted for inflation)
- K **Inflation Factor** the inflation between now and when you retire (from Table 6.1)
  The table has factors for 3% and 4% inflation; use the 3% column as default
- L **Income Needed from Nestegg at Retirement** (J times K)
  In retirement year dollars (adjusted for inflation)

Nestegg

- M **Nestegg Multiplier** from Table 6.3 for a $1.00 withdrawal at 6%, 5% or 4% w/d rate.
  If you're not sure, use 6% for now (16.67).
- N **Nestegg Required at Retirement** (L times M)
  The nestegg you will need when you retire. In retirement age dollars
  - O **Existing Nestegg**
    Your total nestegg today, in current dollars.
  - P **Existing Nestegg Growth Multiplier** from Table 6.7
    The multiplier for growth of a $1.00 nestegg with no add'l investments
    for the number of years until retirement at a rate of return
    from 8% to 12%; if you're not sure use 10% for now.
  - Q **Existing Nestegg at Retirement** (O times P)
    The estimated size of your existing nestegg at retirement
    in retirement year dollars, with no additional investments
- R **Nestegg Shortfall** without additional investment (N minus Q)
  The additional nestegg needed to retire

Investment Required to Eliminate Nestegg Shortfall

- S **Required Investment Divisor** from Table 6.5
  This is the amount that one dollar invested each year would grow to at retirement.
  Enter the amount from Table 6.5 that corresponds to the number years to retirement
  and the rate of return you expect to achieve in your nestegg portfolio.
  If you're not sure, use 10% for now.
- T **Required Annual Investment** (R divided by S)
  This is the amount you need to invest each year until you retire.
- U **Savings and investment as % of earnings** (T divided by D)
  Most people will need to save and invest between 15% and 20%
  of their current earnings in order to retire early or well.
  If that seems like a lot, read the next chapter on lifestyle overhead!

TABLE 6.7   EXISTING NESTEGG GROWTH MULTIPLIER
(Growth of $1.00 Portfolio with no additional investment)

Total Return		8%	9%	10%	11%	12%
Year	1	1.08	1.09	1.10	1.11	1.12
	2	1.17	1.19	1.21	1.23	1.25
	3	1.26	1.30	1.33	1.37	1.40
	4	1.36	1.41	1.46	1.52	1.57
	5	1.47	1.54	1.61	1.69	1.76
	6	1.59	1.68	1.77	1.87	1.97
	7	1.71	1.83	1.95	2.08	2.21
	8	1.85	1.99	2.14	2.30	2.48
	9	2.00	2.17	2.36	2.56	2.77
	10	2.16	2.37	2.59	2.84	3.11
	11	2.33	2.58	2.85	3.15	3.48
	12	2.52	2.81	3.14	3.50	3.90
	13	2.72	3.07	3.45	3.88	4.36
	14	2.94	3.34	3.80	4.31	4.89
	15	3.17	3.64	4.18	4.78	5.47
	16	3.43	3.97	4.59	5.31	6.13
	17	3.70	4.33	5.05	5.90	6.87
	18	4.00	4.72	5.56	6.54	7.69
	19	4.32	5.14	6.12	7.26	8.61
	20	4.66	5.60	6.73	8.06	9.65
	21	5.03	6.11	7.40	8.95	10.80
	22	5.44	6.66	8.14	9.93	12.10
	23	5.87	7.26	8.95	11.03	13.55
	24	6.34	7.91	9.85	12.24	15.18
	25	6.85	8.62	10.83	13.59	17.00
	26	7.40	9.40	11.92	15.08	19.04
	27	7.99	10.25	13.11	16.74	21.32
	28	8.63	11.17	14.42	18.58	23.88
	29	9.32	12.17	15.86	20.62	26.75
	30	10.06	13.27	17.45	22.89	29.96
	31	10.87	14.46	19.19	25.41	33.56
	32	11.74	15.76	21.11	28.21	37.58
	33	12.68	17.18	23.23	31.31	42.09
	34	13.69	18.73	25.55	34.75	47.14
	35	14.79	20.41	28.10	38.57	52.80
	36	15.97	22.25	30.91	42.82	59.14
	37	17.25	24.25	34.00	47.53	66.23
	38	18.63	26.44	37.40	52.76	74.18
	39	20.12	28.82	41.14	58.56	83.08
	40	21.72	31.41	45.26	65.00	93.05

These calculations assume that all of your investment will be in tax-deferred accounts. This is probably okay because the impact of any taxes will probably be offset by increased earnings (and savings/investment potential) in the out-years. Social Security benefits before age 62 can be entered only if additional income from other sources, such as consulting, will replace it.

The worksheet can also be used for any special future needs such as children's education or house downpayment. For many, if not most of us, children's educational needs will preclude full contributions to retirement accounts in at least some years. But if you save less for retirement when you are young, you will need to save more later. This in fact may be a very reasonable choice for many – save a small percentage in your 30's, more in your 40's and more yet in your 50's. A combination of this laddered savings scheme and your naturally higher earnings as you grow older may allow you to reach your goals – gracefully. But don't put off saving!

Table 6.8 below, uses Social Security benefit information from table 39.3 to fill out some of the details of savings and retirement scenarios for our five hypothetical workers at retirement age 55, 62, 65 and 70.

TABLE 6.8   RETIREMENT AGE ANALYSIS FOR FIVE HYPOTHETICAL WORKERS
Current Age 35 (with no nestegg to date)

	A	B	C	D	E
Current Earnings	$32,000	$50,000	$80,000	120,000	250,000
Retirement Budget %	90%	90%	90%	90%	90%
Retirement Budget	$28,800	$45,000	$72,000	$108,000	225,000
	Pension	0	0	0	0
RETIREMENT AT AGE 55					
Social Security	10,020	12,840	13,800	13,800	13,800
Social Security (spouse)	5,010	6,420	6,900	6,900	6,900
Total Social Security	15,030	19,260	20,700	20,700	20,700
Required Income from Nestegg	13,770	25,740	51,300	87,300	204,300
Inflation Factor	1.81	1.81	1.81	1.81	1.81
Req'd Income at Retirement	24,924	46,589	92,853	158,013	369,783
Nestegg Multiplier (at 6%)	16.67	16.67	16.67	16.67	16.67
Req'd Nestegg at Retirement	415,478	776,645	1,547,860	2,634,077	6,164,283
Req'd Investment Amt. Multiplier	99.33	99.33	99.33	99.33	99.33
Req'd Annual Investment	4,183	7,819	15,583	26,518	62,059
Savings % of Earnings	**13.07%**	**15.64%**	**19.48%**	**22.10%**	**24.82%**
RETIREMENT AT AGE 62					
Social Security	10,260	13,320	15,000	15,000	15,000
Social Security (spouse)	5,130	6,660	7,500	7,500	7,500
Total Social Security	15,390	19,980	22,500	22,500	22,500
Required Income from Nestegg	13,410	25,020	49,500	85,500	202,500
Inflation Factor	2.22	2.22	2.22	2.22	2.22
Req'd Income at Retirement	29,770	55,544	109,890	189,810	449,550
Nestegg Multiplier (at 6%)	16.67	16.67	16.67	16.67	16.67
Req'd Nestegg at Retirement	496,269	925,925	1,831,866	3,164,133	7,494,000
Req'd Investment Amt. Multiplier	122.29	122.29	122.29	122.29	122.29
Req'd Annual Investment	4,058	7,572	14,980	25,874	61,280
Savings % of Earnings	**12.68%**	**15.14%**	**18.72%**	**21.56%**	**24.51%**
RETIREMENT AT AGE 65					
Social Security	13,680	17,820	20,040	20,040	20,040
Social Security (spouse)	6,840	8,910	10,020	10,020	10,020
Total Social Security	20,520	26,730	30,060	30,060	30,060
Required Income from Nestegg	8,280	18,270	41,940	77,940	194,940
Inflation Factor	2.43	2.43	2.43	2.43	2.43
Req'd Income at Retirement	20,120	44,396	101,914	189,394	473,704
Nestegg Multiplier (at 6%)	16.67	16.67	16.67	16.67	16.67
Req'd Nestegg at Retirement	335,407	740,083	1,698,910	3,157,201	7,896,649
Req'd Investment Amt. Multiplier	166.08	166.08	166.08	166.08	166.08
Req'd Annual Investment	2,020	4,456	10,229	19,010	47,547
Savings % of Earnings	**6.31%**	**8.91%**	**12.79%**	**15.84%**	**19.01%**
RETIREMENT AT AGE 70					
Social Security	17,760	24,240	26,040	26,040	26,040
Social Security (spouse)	8,880	12,120	13,020	13,020	13,020
Total Social Security	26,640	36,360	39,060	39,060	39,060
Required Income from Nestegg	2,160	8,640	32,940	68,940	185,940
Inflation Factor	2.81	2.81	2.81	2.81	2.81
Req'd Income at Retirement	6,070	24,278	92,561	193,721	522,491
Nestegg Multiplier (at 6%)	16.67	16.67	16.67	16.67	16.67
Req'd Nestegg at Retirement	101,180	404,721	1,542,999	3,229,336	8,709,932
Req'd Investment Amt. Multiplier	273.58	273.58	273.58	273.58	273.58
Req'd Annual Investment	370	1,479	5,640	11,804	31,837
Savings % of Earnings	**1.16%**	**2.96%**	**7.05%**	**9.84%**	**12.73%**

Several important observations from the data in Table 6.8:

Reduced Savings for later retirement

The later you are willing to retire, the less you appear to need to be saving each year to fund your retirement. But there is a trap. If you decide to save next to nothing and live high on the hog before retirement you are betting on good health and continued good earnings. What would happen if health problems precluded continued work? The answer, you would be forced to depend much more on Social Security and be much poorer in retirement than you were planning for. An aggressive savings program before retirement will **always** give you more freedom and better choices later.

Larger variation in required savings for the average (A) worker

There is a much larger variation in the required savings percentage for the average worker (A) than on the more wealthy (D) & (E). The average worker (A) ranges from 13.07% for age 55 retirement to 1.16% at age 70 (over a tenfold difference). The wealthier worker (D) ranges from around 10% to over 20% and (E) ranges from around 12.50% to 25.00% (only about a twofold difference).

The wealthy benefit less from Social Security

On a percentage basis the wealthy benefit far less from Social Security than the average worker. Social Security replaces so much less income for the wealthy workers that their savings must be increased fairly dramatically for any retirement age (vs the average worker). The following table shows the percentage of retirement income each of our hypothetical workers is getting from Social Security at various retirement ages.

TABLE 6.9   **PERCENTAGE OF RETIREMENT BUDGET FROM SOCIAL SECURITY**
(note: the age 55 retirees cannot receive Social Security until age 62)

		A	B	C	D	E
Age	55	52%	43%	29%	19%	9%
	62	53%	44%	31%	21%	10%
	65	71%	59%	42%	28%	13%
	70	93%	81%	54%	36%	17%

If you are not saving 15% you will not be retiring early; and Retirement at 55 requires a lot of savings

This table points out that the 15% savings rule works only very generally. It would allow the average worker (A) to retire at 55; worker (B) at 62; worker (C) between 62 and 65; and worker (D) & (E) would have to work past 65 (or retire on less).

To assure early retirement the average worker can save 15%, the more wealthy (C) & (D) workers need around 20% to retire early. The very wealthy (E) requires close to 25% savings.

How much luxury can you afford now and still retire early or well? The next chapter provides some lifestyle overhead analysis.

Chapter 7
Lifestyle Overhead

> Abstract - Lifestyle Overhead (the luxuries we consume today) is enjoyed at the cost of reduced nestegg accumulation (meaning later or less comfortable retirement). Live well within your means if you want to retire early.

The luxuries (small and large) that we consume today directly and significantly affect what we will have for retirement.

A $10 pizza each month from age 20 to age 65 will reduce the consumer's nestegg at age 65 by $95,000 (See Appendix C for details).

A $10,000 more expensive car every 5 years from age 30 to age 65 will reduce a consumer's nestegg by $725,000 (See Appendix C for details).

That is **the power of compounding**, and most Americans are not taking advantage of it.

The personal savings rate of Americans has dropped steadily from around 8% in the 70's to near zero (or even marginally negative) today; the results speak for themselves. Only a small fraction of the boomers have any chance for the comfortable retirement that most are hoping for. This is the result of their decision (generally subconscious) to consume now and worry about retirement later. It is a very costly decision! You only have two choices of what to do with every penny of every dollar you earn – **spend it <u>now</u> or spend it (and its compounded earnings) <u>later</u>**.

> **Navigation Tip**
> If you are already saving 15% of your gross income, skip the rest of Part 1.

First, stop charging more stuff on your credit cards than you can pay for now. If you are not paying off your credit cards every month, you should cut them up – period! Find a way to live on what you are making and pay off all your credit card debt (work two jobs for a while). Eventually you will have enough to actually start saving.

Second, stop spending every dime you get. If you are not saving, you are living beyond your means – period! The price of a comfortable retirement (or the hope of an early retirement) is simply learning to live well within your means. If you are saving and investing 15% of your gross income you have a reasonable chance to retire comfortably or maybe even retire early if your investments pay off well (or if you turn into a high earner in your out years).

That may sound like a shocking savings goal; to some, it may even sound impossible. It really isn't, but it does require a far lower "lifestyle overhead" than most people realize – not zero, but a lot lower. Think of lifestyle overhead as all the luxuries you consume that are in excess of the minimum required to provide food, shelter and simple clothing. It is a far smaller budget than most people realize. You can revise these numbers for where you live.

TABLE 7.1 THE "BARE MINIMUM" FOR A FAMILY OF FOUR	monthly	yearly
Housing (without any luxury)	$650	$7,800
Food (for simple sustenance)	350	4,200
Transportation (bus or cheap car)	175	2,100
Health Care (health maintenance)	175	2,100
Other Necessities (Clothing & Misc.)	250	3,000
Total	$1,600	$19,200

The 2002 HHS Poverty Guideline was $18,100 per year for a family of four. Everything over say $19,000 is lifestyle overhead. Everything we spend beyond that level (or the similar level appropriate for where you live) is lifestyle overhead. Very few of us will choose to live at the poverty level in order to provide for our retirement, but 85% of your gross income is likely to provide for a fair amount of lifestyle (luxury).

So let's adjust that "Bare Minimum" budget up a little to provide some elbow room for comfort – say by 20%

TABLE 7.2   THE "ADJUSTED BARE MINIMUM" (for 4)

	monthly	yearly
"Bare Minimum" Budget	$1,600	$19,200
20% increase	320	3,840
New "Comfortable Bare Minimum" Budget	$1,920	$23,040

Some lifestyle overhead is reasonable – nobody (well almost nobody anyway) wants to save every penny. But cutting back a little now to allow an early or far more comfortable retirement later is a good trade off.

Looking back at the hypothetical worker examples in the last chapter, remember that the average worker (average according to the Social Security Administration) was earning $32,000 per year and needed to be saving $4,058 per year (12.68% of his earnings) to be able to retire at 62. Lower lifestyle overhead is the only way he can succeed in saving.

TABLE 7.3   ADJUSTED BARE MIN with MAXIMIZED SAVINGS

	monthly	yearly
Total Earnings	$2,667	$32,000
"Comfortable Bare Minimum" spending	1,920	23,040
Taxes (assuming 5% state income tax)	320	4,288
Savings and Investments	$389	$4,672
Savings % of Earning		14.60%

I'm not suggesting that it will be easy for the average family to save 15% – it will not. And the peer pressures for all of you will be relentless. Living with less is hard enough for a couple, but kids add a whole new dimension to spending pressure. I can't tell you how many times our kids complained that they "needed" more expensive tennis shoes (or some other of life's necessities). Today, they understand and appreciate what we did together; but at the time, they just thought we were cheap!

If you are borrowing at your maximums, you are living beyond your means – period! Don't let the bank loan officer mislead you! What can you actually afford to borrow is far less than the bank will loan you for your house and car. If you are not saving 15% you are consuming your retirement (or choosing not to retire). You are giving up the freedom to choose retirement, even if you think you will want to continue to work.

Child care costs require a separate analysis. Many two income families would be better off if they forewent the extra income and eliminated all the extra costs (and stress) associated with it. Do the math – **carefully!** It's not just the cost of child care; it's extra transportation, convenience foods, eating out more (because you're tired) – it adds up to a lot more than most two income families realize. If both are high earners, it's another story. But if the second income is a low wage, it may not make much sense.

You will either learn now how to live within your means, with a more moderate lifestyle overhead; or you will be forced to learn in retirement how to live at something far closer to subsistence than you were hoping for.

Chapter 8
Saving

> Abstract - If you are not saving enough today, you need to create a savings discipline. Automatic payroll deduction may be just what you need. You can also add part (or all) of your future raises to savings until you reach your saving rate goal.

You already know that you need to be saving for retirement, and once a year you and most other Americans vow to save more next year (and lose weight, eat better and exercise more). On average, very little happens, and the procrastination is very costly (on all counts). We seem to need a missing discipline to trick us into saving.

How come? Well, a new science called behavioral finance tells us that when it comes to savings, investment and retirement planning, we do not behave rationally. We know what we need to do; we just don't do it.

How can we overcome this irrational inertia?

New research by Richard Thaler, of the University of Chicago, points toward a potential solution. **Make the inertia work for you.** His plan involves making enrollment in an employer savings plan automatic (requiring a written request to withdraw from the plan). In addition, employees agree to contribute a portion of all future raises to additional savings (again requiring a written request to reduce additional savings).

Experiments with this plan have produced remarkable results. Enrollment in savings plans increased from around 49% to around 86%; and savings rates increased from 3% of gross salaries to around 11%.

If your employer doesn't offer such a plan, you can still create a similar discipline on your own.

First. If you aren't already contributing to a savings or retirement plan, start contributing at least a little. Whether it's $10 a week, 1% of your gross salary, or the maximum allowed, start savings some amount each week. You can create a significant discipline by establishing an automatic payroll deduction to be deposited to your bank (and transferred to your IRA or other investment account). Check with your employer and bank regarding your options.

Second. Add some of every future raise to this automatic deduction. I suggest you consider adding at least one-third (if not all) of your future raises to savings (until you reach your savings rate goal).

Once you are saving enough, your task then changes to investing it well.

Part Two

Investment Basics

Chapter 9
Capitalism and Free Enterprise
The Engines of Wealth Creation

> Abstract - Capitalism continues to create new wealth (the world economy is growing); the way to participate is to invest in it (both in the U.S. and in global markets).

Raw entrepreneurship is the real engine of wealth creation.

We all know stories of the spectacular financial success of dynamic entrepreneurs like my last employer, Marshall Erdman. He came to the U.S. from Lithuania in the 30's with $17. He built one of the largest and most innovative design-build companies in the country, amassed a significant personal fortune and provided for the livelihood of about 1000 families.

In every community in the U.S. there are dozens of similar stories of success. "The Millionaire Next Door" documents that there are quiet millionaires in all of our communities both large and small. They are the risk takers in small businesses everywhere. These small business opportunities, sometimes started with little more than sweat equity or by risking everything, have the highest rate of return of **all** possible investments; and therefore carry extraordinary risk – the risk of total failure and bankruptcy.

We are lucky to live in America. It truly is the land of opportunity, and the closer we get to its entrepreneurship, the higher our potential returns. I was fortunate to participate in the ownership of several businesses in the last 30 years. Some are no longer in business; some were successful; some were very successful. Those of us lucky enough to have significant ownership in successful small companies have accumulated wealth more rapidly than average.

But all of us can participate in the miracle of capitalism and free enterprise. If you don't have ownership of a small closely held private business, then you should by all means possible (except borrowing) invest in the stock market. Whether we have ownership in a small closely held company, own the publicly traded stocks of corporations in the U.S. and around the world, or simply own mutual funds, we are expressing faith in the growth of the U.S. and world economies.

Over the last 75 years these markets have returned a little more than 7% over inflation. Investments in these markets will form a key part of your investment strategy. But the game has changed in the last 50 years, you can no longer expect to beat the market just because you have the advice of a professional money manager or stock broker.

The academic research of the last 50 years has documented that individuals and professionals alike are failing, on average, to beat the market. The stock picking, market timing and mutual fund chasing strategies of active management no longer work.

Chapter 10
Active Management
The Loser's Game in an Efficient Market

Abstract - The Efficient Market Theory holds that things have changed in the last 50 years. The market can no longer be beaten by doing research and getting good advice. The market has become well-informed professionals competing with other well-informed professionals and all new information is absorbed immediately. The costs of trying to beat the market cannot be overcome. Trying to beat the market is a loser's game.

> **Navigation Tip**
> If you don't want to dig through the research that debunks Wall Street and their stock picking and market timing strategies (active management) you can reread the abstracts in the rest of Part 2 and go on to Part 3, Chapter 18, Modern Portfolio Theory. Come back and read this section later; you need to know this stuff to defend yourself against Wall Street advertising, misinformation and obfuscation.

The conventional wisdom is that the active management strategies of **stock picking, market timing** and **mutual fund picking** are the ways to succeed in investing. They may have worked 30 years ago but they don't work any more. Wall Street claims that this game can be won; but the truth is, it has become a loser's game.

> *"The 'money game' we call investment management has evolved in recent decades from a winner's game to a loser's game. A basic change has occurred in the investment environment; the market came to be dominated in the 1970's by the very institutions that were striving to outperform the market. In just 30 years, the market activities of the investing institutions shifted from only 10 percent of the total public transactions to an overwhelming 90 percent. And that shift made all the difference. No longer was the active manager competing against cautious custodians or amateurs who were out of touch with the market; now he or she was competing with other experts."*
>
> Charles Ellis, The Loser's Game, p 4

In order to compete successfully with these experts, an investor must regularly find mispriced securities to buy or sell at a profit.

> *"The pickers and timers of active management don't believe markets work. They think prices adjust slowly enough that they can systematically uncover incorrectly priced securities and add value beyond added management and trading costs."*
>
> John J. Bowen and Daniel C. Goldie
> Prudent Investor's Guide, p 21

Let's look at how quickly markets respond to new information. In **fixed income markets** information is assimilated so quickly that market *"adjustment to announcements regarding interest rates, employment and inflation data begins within ten seconds of the news release and are basically over within 40 seconds of the release."* What kind of chance do you really think you have to get in on that action?

Ederington and Lee, Journal of Financial and Quantitative Anaylsis, March 1995

Research indicates that the **equities markets** are so efficient in incorporating news and announcements into valuations that it is futile to try to beat it. The majority of the price response to overnight news and announcements is realized during the opening trade (for both NYSE and NASDAQ). Valuation adjustments from daytime news and announcements are realized during the first trade following the announcement on the NASDAQ and take only a few trades on the NYSE.

Jason T. Green & Susan G. Watts
Price Discovery on the NYSE and NASDAQ
Financial Management, Spring 1996

Eugene F. Fama coined the phrase "efficient Market" in explaining how markets appear to absorb new information so that the current price reflects all known information. Every stock is looked at by at least dozens, if not hundreds, of professionals. Finding one that hasn't already been considered by others is nearly impossible.

> *"In a real way, the very skill, quality and access and number of people doing the research limits the value of the process. ...with so many players, the point of diminishing return may be far behind us."*
>
> Frank Armstrong, Investment Strategies for the 21st Century

> *"The securities market is an open, free, and competitive market in which large numbers of well-informed and price-sensitive investors and professional investment managers compete skillfully, vigorously, and continuously as both buyers and sellers. Non-experts can easily retain the services of experts. Prices are quoted widely and promptly. Effective prohibitions against market manipulations are established. And arbitrageurs, traders, market technicians, and longer-term 'fundamental investors' seek to find and profit from any market imperfections. Such a market is considered efficient. ...Not perfect, and not even perfectly efficient, but sufficiently efficient that wise investors will not expect to be able to exploit its inefficiencies regularly."*
>
> Charles Ellis, The Loser's Game, p 18

The market is efficient enough that stocks with high expectations have high prices (by any number of measures). The only question is whether the company will do better or worse than expected. In order to make money on the stock, the company must do better than everyone else is expecting (not just do well) in the future. That's often not a good bet. But the market does get exuberant about certain stocks from time to time and a great deal of money can be made (theoretically) by investing in companies for which the news in the future is better than was expected. But that's the rub; the news is by definition random. If you really knew what was going to happen in the future, you wouldn't be reading this book.

> *"In an efficient market, any new information the market receives will be random, not in the sense of being good or bad, but in the sense of whether or not it surpasses or falls short of market expectations. Whether subsequent information will affect the price of a stock in a negative or positive manner is random."*
>
> Larry Swedroe, The Only Guide to a Winning Investment Strategy
You'll Ever Need, p 65

The fact that stock valuations sometimes move violently does not argue against market efficiency, but rather that new information exceeds or falls short of expectations very significantly. *"The efficient market theory does not claim that the current price is the correct price, only that the market incorporates everything that is known about a stock (including forecasts of future earnings, etc.) into its current valuation or price."*

Larry Swedroe, The Only Guide to a Winning Investment Strategy
You'll Ever Need, p 65

Wall Street sometimes admits that most markets are, in fact, fairly efficient, but then claims that small cap stocks, or international stocks, or finally emerging market stocks are traded in relatively inefficient markets. This turns out to be half true, but the cost of trading in these markets is so much higher that the inefficiency doesn't matter. See the discussion of turnover and trading costs that follows in Chapter 13.

The real question is not whether or not the market is efficient or just how efficient it may or may not be. The question is rather, can you overcome all of the costs of trying to beat it. The evidence is overwhelming that neither you, nor most money managers, are able to overcome the costs, and these costs are far larger than most people suspect.

If you listen to Wall Street and the financial media, you get the impression that "beating the market" is simply a matter of getting good advice and applying it. But academic research has shown that most funds and money managers fail to overcome the cost hurdle of transaction costs, fees, and management expenses. In addition, the research has consistently shown that those who do beat the averages do so randomly.

Michael Jensen was among the first to look carefully at the performance of mutual funds. He studied the performance of 115 mutual funds from 1945 to 1964. He published studies in 1968 and 1969 documenting the risk adjusted performance of these funds (56 funds had data back to 1945; all 115 had data from 1955 on). Jensen utilized the concept of "alpha" to measure risk-adjusted performance. Alpha is a measure of the return of a fund in excess of a benchmark. A negative alpha is underperformance.

> *"It appears from the preponderance of negative alphas that the funds were not able to forecast security prices well enough to recover their research expenses, management fees and commissions."*
>
> Michael Jensen, The Performance of Mutual Funds
> from 1945-1964, Journal of Finance, May 1968 p 406

> *"One must realize that these analysts are extremely well endowed. Moreover, they operate in the securities market every day and have wide ranging contacts in both the business and financial communities. Thus, the fact that they are apparently not able to forecast returns accurately enough to recover their research and transaction costs is a striking piece of evidence in favor of the strong [efficient market] hypothesis."*
>
> Michael Jensen, Journal of Business, April 1969, p 170

Far fewer mutual funds beat their benchmarks each year than we are led to believe, and to make matters worse their past performance doesn't seem to matter. The next chapter looks at the actual performance of mutual funds.

Chapter 11
Actual Mutual Fund Performance and Persistence of Performance
(good past performance does not persist into the future)

Abstract - Research indicates that very few mutual funds beat their benchmarks each year, that those doing so appear to be random, and that good past performance does not persist into the future. Nobody can guess which mutual funds will do well in the future. On average, mutual funds trail their benchmarks by the total of all their costs and expenses.

Each year there is new list of the best mutual funds (from last year). If there was strong persistence of past performance into the future, these lists would look a lot more alike year after year. The painful truth is that these lists are almost useless, because next year it's going to be a whole new bunch.

The fact that nearly **one-third** of the mutual funds existing since 1961 have disappeared is not mentioned in the ads. The fact that "average" surviving mutual fund performance is increased due to the exclusion of these "dead" funds from the data is not mentioned in any ads. When a mutual fund is doing so badly that it cannot recover, it ceases business either by dissolving or being absorbed into other funds in a group. Survivorship bias (the upward bias of returns data because of the exclusion of failed funds) is a term of the scholarship of finance. It is one of Wall Street's secrets.

A landmark study by Mark Carhart reviewed the performance of all known equity funds (adjusted for survivorship bias) from 1962-1993. His data set included 1,892 funds. From 1962 to 1993, 582 of the funds had disappeared. Carhart concluded:

> "... that persistence in mutual fund performance is almost totally explained by differences in fund expenses and transaction costs, rather than the superior stock picking or market timing skills of the managers."
>
> "Winners are somewhat more likely to remain winners, and losers are more likely to remain losers or perish. However, the top decile [the best performing 10% of the funds] differ substantially each year, with **more than 80% turnover** in their composition. In addition, **last years winners frequently become next years losers and vice versa**, which is consistent with **gambling behavior** by mutual funds."
>
> "... the year to year rankings of most funds appear to be random."
>
> "Funds in decile 1 [the best 10% of funds] have a 17% probability of remaining in that decile, and the funds in decile 10 [the worst 10% of funds] have a 46% chance of remaining in decile 10 or disappearing from the sample altogether."
>
> Mark M. Carhart
> On Persistence in Mutual Fund Performance
> Journal of Finance, Mar 97

Mutual Fund ratings such as Morningstar's Star System don't predict future performance. A Lipper Analytical Services study of only Morningstar 5 star funds found that 90 of 94 would have failed to beat the portfolio asset classes.

Larry Swedroe, The Only Guide to a Winning Investment Strategy
You'll Ever Need, p 29

> *"The connection between past and future performance has not been firmly established by stars, historical star ratings, or any raw data."*

John Rekenthaler,
editor of Morningstar Mutual Funds
quoted by Swedroe, The Only Guide to a Winning Investment
Strategy You'll Ever Need, p 29

> *"We never intended to suggest that the stars could be used to predict short term returns or to time fund purchases. They were just a way to sort funds according to past success"*

Morningstar Mutual Funds, 12/8/95
quoted by Swedroe, The Only Guide to a Winning Investment
Strategy You'll Ever Need, p 29, 30

It is estimated that 80% of new fund purchases are four and five star ranked funds. Apparently, not many investors know that Morningstar ratings have no predictive value.

Kipplinger Personal Finance, Feb 97
quoted by Swedroe, The Only Guide to a Winning Investment
Strategy You'll Ever Need, p 30

Michael Jensen, in his 1969 study, found <u>no</u> significant evidence that *"a fund manager who experienced superior performance in the earlier period was far more likely to experience superior results in the later period."* On the other hand, he did find that *"a fund which was inferior in the earlier period was very likely to be inferior in the later period."* He then continues with an observation that caused me to laugh out loud (very rare in the stacks of the UW Business School):

> *"This result is not too surprising, since it is very simple to consistently hold an inferior portfolio. In the absence of forecasting ability all one need do is generate substantial expenses through time to insure inferior performance."*

Michael Jensen, Journal of Business, April 1969, p 236

The negative contribution of expenses can hardly be overemphasized. Carhart observes that *"mutual fund managers claim that expenses and turnover do not reduce performance, since investors are paying for the quality of the manager's information, and because managers trade only to increase expected returns net of transaction costs."* That's their claim anyway; their results appear to indicate that they are overconfident. He found that their *"expense ratios, portfolio turnover and load fees are significantly and negatively related to performance."*

Mark M. Carhart
On Persistence in Mutual Fund Performance
Journal of Finance, Mar 97, p 80

The next chapters look by turn at the costs associated with operating expenses, turnover and trading costs, the index fund advantage and distributions and taxes.

Chapter 12
Mutual Fund Operating Expenses

Abstract - Mutual fund operating expenses are a serious drag on their performance. The higher the expenses the poorer the performance.

Proponents of active management claim that informed investors (mutual fund managers in particular) earn enough to compensate for the cost of gathering and analyzing information. These expenses are reflected in their published expense ratios. But Mark Carhart found that:

> *"Most funds underperform by about the magnitude of their investment expenses. The bottom decile funds [the worst 10% of funds], however, underperform by about twice their reported investment costs.*
>
> Mark M. Carhart
> On Persistence in Mutual Fund Performance
> Journal of Finance, Mar 97, p 80

The Elton and Gruber study of 143 mutual funds from 1965 to 1984 showed a strong inverse relationship between cost and performance. The benchmark for each fund was a portfolio of indexes reflecting each fund's individual exposure to S&P 500, small cap and bonds. The resulting "alpha" for each fund reflects their risk adjusted performance compared to the fund benchmark. Not only did the funds as a whole underperform the indexes, the more expensive the fund is, the worse it performs.

TABLE 12.1   ELTON & GRUBER EXPENSE vs. PERFORMANCE

Quintile	Expenses	Alpha
5 (high)	0.912 to 2.020	-3.87%
4	0.753 to 0.912	-1.68%
3	0.680 to 0.753	-0.69%
2	0.590 to 0.680	-1.19%
1 (low)	0.000 to 0.590	-0.59%

Edwin J. Elton, Martin J. Gruber, et al
Efficiency with Costly Information:
Society for Financial Studies, 1993

The facts are simple, fund expenses have a negative impact on fund performance, the higher the expenses, the worse the performance. Index funds have lower expenses because they are not trying to beat the market; they simply buy and hold the market (or market segment) and therefore perform closer to their benchmarks.

Solution – find the index fund (for the asset class you want to hold) with the lowest expenses.

In addition to operating expenses, some funds charge 12b-1 fees, front-end loads or deferred sales charges. Be careful to understand all of these fees and loads – they cost you real money. Since load funds have not out-performed no-load funds, there is no good reason to pay these fees and loads. There are plenty of good no-load funds available to choose from.

The only exception is the fee for redemption in less than three to five years that some funds use to limit trading and attract buy-and-hold investors.

Chapter 13
Turnover and Trading Costs

Abstract - The trading costs associated with the turnover of mutual funds is an important (unreported) overhead for the funds. In addition, higher turnover is directly related to poorer performance. The trading costs in small cap funds is particularly high. Active management only makes things worse. The Average turnover of actively managed mutual funds is 85%; the turnover of passively managed index funds is typically less than 10%.

Active fund managers (the stock pickers and market timers) do a lot of trading. The average retail mutual fund has a turnover rate of 85%; which means that they replace 85% of their holdings each year with new holdings.

High turnover is costly to fund shareholders because of the trading costs associated with commissions, bid-ask spreads and market impact costs. These costs are a hidden drag on the performance of a mutual fund – in addition to its published expenses. Trading costs for small cap stock funds can exceed management fees. While less for large cap stock stocks, they are always significant.

Trading costs are closely related to the bid-ask spread, the difference between the asking price (the price at which a stock is bought by a broker for an investor) and the bid price (at which it is sold by a broker to an investor). This "spread" is the fee charged by the market makers; it is their overhead and profit – the cost of liquidity in our markets.

The trading volume for large cap stocks like IBM, GE and Walmart is very high (very many trades each day), so the profit and overhead for each trade remains very small (they make it up in volume). But the volume of trading for relatively unknown and unfollowed small and micro cap stocks is very low (sometimes no trades at all in a given day), so the profit and overhead for each trade is far higher (there is no volume to make it up on).

The bid-ask spread is nearly 12 times greater for stocks in the smallest CRSP (Center for Research on Securities Pricing) decile than for the largest decile. CRSP deciles represent the whole market divided by size according to market capitalization. See Chapter 23 for additional details regarding CRSP deciles.

TABLE 13.1   U.S. MARKET BID-ASK-SPREAD

Decile	Bid-ask-spread
1 (large cap)	0.53%
2	0.60%
3 (mid cap)	0.71%
4	0.98%
5	1.25%
6 (small cap)	1.26%
7	1.61%
8	2.21%
9 (micro cap)	2.99%
10	6.19%

The bid-ask spreads in international markets are even higher.

As a rule-of-thumb you can estimate the trading cost of a fund by multiplying its turnover rate by its average bid-ask spread (the percentage spread for its average size holding). For the average mid-cap fund this amounts to

> 85% turnover x 1.25% bid-ask spread, or a **1.08%** drag on performance **in addition to its published expenses!**

The turnover in index funds is far smaller, ranging from 1% to no more than 25%, depending on the asset class — say 10%.

> 10% turnover for passive funds x 1.25% bid-ask-spread would be only **0.125%** (1/8 of one percent instead of over one percent)

The average trading costs for active, passive, large, mid and small cap funds may be summarized as follows. The following estimates of trading costs are based on an average active turnover of 85% for active funds and 10% for passive index funds, and the bid-ask spreads from the table above.

TABLE 13.2   ESTIMATES OF TRADING COSTS FOR FUNDS

	Bid-Ask Spread	ACTIVE 85% turnover	PASSIVE INDEX 10% turnover
Deciles 1&2 large cap	0.57%	85%x0.57%= **0.48%**	10%x0.57%= **0.06%**
Deciles 3-5 mid cap	0.98%	85%x0.98%= **0.83%**	10%x0.98%= **0.10%**
Deciles 6-8 small cap	1.61%	85%x1.61%= **1.37%**	10%x1.61%= **0.16%**
Deciles 9-10 micro cap	4.59%	85%x4.59%= **3.90%**	10%x4.59%= **0.46%**

These differences form a significant hurdle for active managers. Most fail to clear it.

In addition to paying the bid-ask spread, a large trade (one that is a significant percentage of the daily trading volume of a stock) is likely to influence the price. This market impact cost adds additional cost to the transaction (making winners more expensive to buy and losers into bigger losers).

The Elton and Gruber study of mutual funds also showed an inverse relationship between turnover and performance — the higher the turnover, the worse the performance.

TABLE 13.3   ELTON & GRUBER TURNOVER vs. PERFORMANCE

Quintile	Turnover	Alpha
5 (high)	72% to 162%	-2.21%
4	51% to 72%	-1.87%
3	34% to 51%	-2.17%
2	22% to 34%	-1.11%
1 (low)	0% to 22%	-0.58%

Edwin J. Elton, Martin J. Gruber, et al
Efficiency with Costly Information:
Society for Financial Studies, 1993

In addition, heavily advertised high turnover funds penalize buy-and-hold investors. The "hot money" that chases last year's returns and then sells on any "alarming" drop in value, can sell at net asset value — effectively free from the long term costs of high turnover. Long term buy-and-hold investors are left holding the bag.

The facts again are simple. High turnover has a negative impact on fund performance. The solution — find the index funds with the lowest possible turnover and fees.

Chapter 14
The Index Fund Advantage

Abstract - The low expenses of index funds provide a huge advantage.

There's a lot more to index funds today than the S&P 500 funds that dominate attention. The Vanguard 500 Index Fund is today the largest mutual fund in the world, and there are numerous other S&P 500 index funds available. The S&P 500 is by far the most popular index around which index funds are constructed, and it remains an important proxy for the market as a whole.

But there are many other kinds of index funds, and numerous other indexes around which new funds are being built each year. Individuals now have available to them numerous index funds that track all manner of important segments such as small cap, value, international and emerging markets.

The first index fund (started in 1971) was available only to institutional investors; other institutional funds followed in 1973, and then in 1975 John Bogle and the Vanguard Group offered the first retail index fund to individuals.

The growth of indexing since then has been in response to strong and growing demand for alternatives to the failed active management strategies of most mutual funds. The index fund advantage is that it assures at least very close to market returns, by minimizing the expenses involved in mutual fund investing.

The following table compares the expenses of both actively managed mutual funds and index funds in three important general asset classes.

TABLE 14.1 ACTIVE FUND VS INDEX FUND EXPENSES

	Large Cap	Small Cap & Int'l	Emerging Markets
Active Fund Expenses			
Expenses Ratio	1.30%	1.60%	2.00%
Trading Costs	0.48%	1.37%	3.00%
Impact Costs	0.30%	1.00%	3.00%
Total Active Fund Expenses	2.08%	3.97%	8.00%
Index Fund Expenses			
Expenses Ratio	0.17%	0.27%	0.57%
Trading Costs	0.06%	0.16%	0.40%
Impact Costs	0.02%	0.15%	0.40%
Total Index Fund Expenses	0.25%	0.58%	1.37%
The Index Fund Advantage	1.83%	3.39%	6.63%

The total expenses of actively managed funds are a significant headwind against which active managers constantly strain. Their failure to demonstrate stock picking or market timing skills adequate to recover these costs is now well documented.

The solution – index funds.

"Most investors, both institutional and individual, will find that the best way to own common stocks is through an index fund that charges minimal fees. Those following this path are sure to beat the results (after fees and expenses) delivered by the great majority of investment professionals"

Warren Buffet, Feb 1977,
Letter to Shareholders

"The deterioration of performance by professionals is getting worse. But the public thinks they are doing great because the average fund is up...But, they'd be better off in an index fund"

Peter Lynch

"Hopelessly unpopular with investment managers and with most clients, the uninspiring, dull 'market portfolio' (or 'index fund') is seldom given anything like the respect it deserves. Plodding along in its unimaginative, inexpensive 'no-brainer' way, this 'plain Jane' form of investing will, over time, achieve better results than most professional investment managers."

Charles Ellis, The Loser's Game, p 17

Don't sell a simple index fund strategy short.

Chapter 15
Distributions and Taxes

> Abstract - Individual taxes (income and capital gains taxes) on mutual fund distributions can cause your personal return from a fund to be far lower than its published return (sometimes only half). Taxable investment performance must be evaluated on an after-tax basis. Taxes are not an issue in an IRA or 401K.

Mutual funds must distribute 98% of their taxable income each year (or pay huge additional taxes). The resulting distributions create taxable income for fund shareholders in the form of dividends, interest and capital gains. This is very important for your taxable investment accounts. But funds do not tend to publish much after-tax data, because it is such bad news!

Studies indicate that the average taxable investor in actively managed funds (who reinvests all distributions) ends up with only 45% to 55% of a fund's published performance after taxes.

> John B. Shoven and Joel M. Dickson
> Ranking Mutual Funds on an After Tax Basis
> Stanford University Center for Economic Policy
> Research, Discussion Paper #344

Robert Arnott's study, "Is Your Alpha Big Enough to Cover Taxes" compared the after-tax performance of actively managed mutual funds with a passively managed index fund. They found that 21% of the funds, 15 out of 72, outperformed the index fund on a pre-tax basis; but only 7%, 5 out of 72, outperformed the index fund after taxes were accounted for.

> Robert H. Jeffrey & Robert D. Arnott
> Is Your Alpha Big Enough to Cover Your Taxes
> Journal of Portfolio Management, spring 93

Subsequent reductions in capital gains tax rates have improved the situation marginally, but taxes remain an important problem for mutual fund investors.

There are horror stories involving distribution and taxes from actively managed mutual funds. Often they involve paying taxes on large distributions while the fund's value has declined. This problem could be exacerbated in a major market crash when a fund must liquidate highly appreciated assets to cover withdrawals. In addition, to assure adequate liquidity for the fund during panic selling, the funds tend to keep cash on hand that dilutes their returns.

You should stay away from heavily advertised funds that attract the "hot money" that is likely to panic in the next downturn and cause you to "receive" large unexpected distributions.

Passively managed funds will generally have far lower distributions. Passively managed funds will always have lower turnover, and that will make their distributions much more stable and predictable. With active managers, you never know when unrealized gains will be realized.

Taxes are not an issue inside an IRA or other tax-deferred account. In these accounts, you can use tax-inefficient funds without penalty.

Chapter 16
Actual Results of Individuals
(much poorer than you think)

> Abstract - Over the last 16 years, individuals, on average, have earned only about 5% per year while the funds they invested in were earning about 16% per year. This poor performance is directly related to bad market timing – chasing the hot funds and panic selling in market declines. Individuals also do poorly as traders of common stocks. On average, the stocks they sell do better than the new stocks they buy after the trade. They would do far better with a simple buy-and-hold strategy, instead of their buy high sell low behavior.

The average individual investor is overconfident – period!

Investors don't want to admit it, but they are not doing well in the market. Studies indicate that individuals owning shares in mutual funds are earning only a very small fraction (20% to 35%) of the published returns of the funds themselves.

What in the world are they doing? How can anyone do THAT bad?

In 1994 Dalbar Financial Services conducted an analysis of results of individual investors in mutual funds as opposed to the published results of the funds themselves. The original Quantitative Analysis of Investor Behavior (The QAIB) covered the period from 1984-1993. The QAIB study has been regularly updated since then and continues to document the awful performance of individuals in mutual funds. Dalbar's summary of the 2001 update states that in the period from January 1984 to December 2000 the average equity fund investor realized an annualized return of 5.32%, compared to 16.29% for the S&P 500 index fund. **The average individual trailed the index by 10.97%**; that is:

> $42,139 growth on $100,000 for individuals (over 16 years), when there was
> $705,847 growth in a $100,000 S&P 500 investment over the same period **(16.8 times more!)**

This extremely poor performance is directly related to bad market timing and short holding periods. Individuals overreact to changing market conditions. And the more an investor buys and sells, the lower the returns.

The QAIB also tracked money flowing into and out of mutual funds and measured the length of time investors remained invested in them. Individuals average fund retention was 2.6 years in 2000 (down from 2.8 in 1999, but up from 1.7 after the stock market crash in 1987). Returns for investors clearly illustrate that they would have benefited from a buy-and-hold strategy. The data indicates that investors invariably buy high and sell low. AFTER the market goes up, cash flows in; AFTER the market goes down, cash flows out.

Stephen Nesbitt looked at individual investments in mutual funds over a 10 year period. He found that despite good performance records for the mutual funds over the period, poor timing of cash flows reduced returns to investors.

> *"Mutual fund cash flows repeatedly go to asset classes near their performance peaks, and leave quickly after returns level off or fall. Unfortunately, the investment industry contributes to this result by heavily advertising products with favorable short term performance."*
>
> Stephen Nesbitt, Journal of Portfolio Management
> Fall 1995, pp 57-60

Investors tend to form a humongous herd that drives the prices of high performing stocks to unrealistic highs and poor performing stocks to unrealistic lows. Investors seem to have an uncanny ability to buy high and sell low.

Terrance Odean analyzed the detailed trading records for a large sample of investors (66,000 households) from a discount brokerage house. **The stocks that individuals sell subsequently outperform the stocks that they buy.**

Terrance Odean, Why Do Investors Trade So Much?
Working Paper, 1977

In a study published later regarding the same data, he looked at the trading behavior and success of these individuals from 1987 to 1993. He found that trading by individual investors is excessive and dysfunctional. He divided the group into quintiles by trading volume. The average household had an annual turnover of 75%; the highest trading quintile had a turnover of over 250%!

> *"Those that trade most earn an annual return of 11.4%, while the market returns 17.9%. ...Overconfidence can explain high trading levels and the resulting poor performance of individual investors."*

Terrance Odean and Brad Barber
Trading is Hazardous to Your Wealth
Journal of Finance, April 2000

In 1995 Morningstar was commissioned by Fundminder, Inc. to evaluate investor returns from mutual fund investments. *"The study evaluated 199 growth mutual funds for which they had performance data for 1989-1994. The average return for the 199 funds over the six year period was 12.01 %. So, how did the individual owners of those same 199 funds do for their various periods of ownership? Not good. The average annualized return was just 2.02%! They turned 12% returns into 2% returns!"*

John Merrill, Beyond Stocks

Either market timing or chasing the hot manager turned their 12 percent return into 2 percent. Buy high, sell low!

> *"Further proof of this finding was provided by Peter Lynch, the highly regarded manager of the Fidelity Magellan Fund during its glory years, who told an audience of investment advisors in 1992: 'Over half of my investors in Fidelity Magellan during my tenure at the helm lost money due to poorly timed buy and sell decisions.' This despite Magellan being the number one performing mutual fund over those 10 years!"*

John Merrill, Beyond Stocks

If buying low is such a good idea, how come so few people do it?

The stock market may well be the only "store" where we refuse to buy good stuff when its on sale and then greedily buy it up when the price goes back up. If you can buy $1.00 bills for 75 cents, who in his right mind would wait until they cost $1.25. A down markets means bargains! If you are in the market, you need to get used to the idea that there are going to be down markets, sometimes for extended periods. The overreaction of individuals to market conditions has been (and for most will continue to be) very costly. If you are adequately diversified into a number of good low cost index funds (say U.S. large, U.S. small and International at a minimum), you can rebalance your investments at the end of each year and in effect buy low and sell high (Chapter 34 contains a discussion of rebalancing). Regular payroll deductions can also help you avoid overreactions to the market.

The next chapter looks at the role of Wall Street and the financial media.

Chapter 17
Wall Street Misinformation Technical and Fundamental Analysis

Abstract - Wall Street and the financial media are still selling active management – stock picking, market timing and mutual fund picking. Their obfuscation of their failure is relentless. Neither fundamental security analysis nor technical analysis works. These guys are guessing, and on average they seem to be right less than half the time; but you will still pay dearly for their advice. Warren Buffet and Peter Lynch both recommend index funds.

Wall Street continues to sell advice about stock picking, market timing and mutual fund picking even though the overwhelming body of research has discredited these strategies. They continue to pander to investors who hope to beat the market by finding the next Microsoft (or the next Warren Buffet or Peter Lynch), or timing the next market moves, up or down. The investment pandering that encourages this hope is shameless and self-serving.

The stock broker calling you with his latest "tip" is not your friend.

> *"Don't be confused about stockbrokers. They are usually very nice people, but their job is not to make money for you. Their job is to make money from you."*

> *"The typical stockbroker 'talks to' 200 customers with invested assets of $5 million. To earn $100,000 a year, he needs to generate $300,000 in gross commissions, or 6% of the money he talks to."*
>
> Charles Ellis, The Loser's Game, p 105

Wall Street maximizes its profits in a number of ways; many do not benefit investors. Buy recommendations far exceed sell recommendations on Wall Street. Why?

> *"There is a darker side to the research problem that investors must also consider. Conflicts of interest can easily creep into analysis. It shouldn't surprise us that buy to sell recommendations is skewed, and that sell recommendations come far too late to be of any use."*
>
> Frank Armstrong, Investment Strategies for the 21st Century, ch 7

The main reason that the majority of individual investors don't know about the last 50 years of research and modern portfolio theory is that the primary business of the financial media is not educating the public; but rather, maximizing their profits. Their advertising revenue comes mainly from financial advisors and mutual funds hawking their stock picking and market timing skills.

Numerous studies of the lists of "the best mutual funds" confirm that they are useless – or worse. The obvious question – why is it a new list every year – remains unanswered. Studies indicate that following this kind of advice is hazardous to your financial wealth.

> *"I believe the search for the top performing stock funds is an intellectually discredited exercise that will come to be viewed as one of the great financial follies of the late 20th century"*
>
> Jonathon Clements,
Wall Street Journal, Apr 29, 1997
quoted by Swedroe, The Only Guide to a Winning Investment
Strategy You'll Ever Need, p 38

Stories of wildly profitable stock picks, market timing calls and mutual funds amount to investment pandering. But that is all you can find in the financial media.

> *"Americans are indulging themselves in investment porn. Shameless stories about performance tickle our prurient financial interest."*
>
> Jane Bryant Quinn, Newsweek, 8/7/95

Wall Street research comes in two basic flavors: technical analysis and fundamental analysis. Neither of these works.

Technical Analysis

Technical analysts used to be called "chartists", but that title has been abandoned. Wall Street uses them to generate trading volume even though their "science" has been thoroughly discredited. Their ability to forecast is non-existent.

Fundamental Analysis

Fundamental analysis is more scientific, but it is still useless for forecasting. Benjamin Graham, the father of fundamental analysis, was interviewed shortly before his death in 1976. Benjamin Graham and David Dodd authored Security Analysis, the bible of fundamental analysts to this day. In the interview he said the following:

> *"I am no longer an advocate of elaborate techniques of security analysis in order to find superior value opportunities. This was a rewarding activity, say forty years ago when our textbook 'Graham and Dodd' [Security Analysis] was first published; but the situation has changed a great deal since then. In the old days any well-trained security analyst could do a professional job of selecting undervalued issues through detailed studies; but in the light of the enormous amount of research now being carried on, I doubt whether such extensive efforts will generate sufficiently superior selection to justify their cost."*
>
> Benjamin Graham Interview
> Financial Analysts Journal
> September/October 1976

A study by two academic researchers found that only 13 of 237 market timing newsletters survived the 12.5 year period of their study.

W. Scott Simon, Index Mutual Funds

The Wall Street Journal conducts a biannual survey of the nation's top Wall Street and professional economists. For the 18 years from 1969 to 1997: 3-mo. T-Bills moved in the opposite direction of the consensus forecast 53% of the time; 30-year Bond consensus was wrong 67% of the time; the more rates moved, the worse the forecasts got (essentially, economists missed 9 of the 10 largest moves in the last 18 years). Only 14 of the 44 (who participated in at least 10 surveys) guessed the right direction 50% of the time; none were accurate more than 60% of the time. Bottom line – **These guys are guessing!**

Journal of Investing, Summer 1997
quoted by Swedroe, The Only Guide to a Winning Investment
Strategy You'll Ever Need, p 90

What Wall Street and the financial media won't tell you is that the smart money has abandoned active management stock picking and market timing. Developed by Nobel Prize winning academics and now utilized by more than half of the institutional money, Modern Portfolio Theory is not well known to the general public.

The next section provides an introduction to Modern Portfolio Theory.

Part Three

Modern Investing

Chapter 18
Modern Portfolio Theory

> Abstract - Modern Portfolio Theory (MPT) has changed the investment landscape. MPT began with the insight of Harry Markowitz in 1952 that portfolio diversification can reduce portfolio volatility (risk) and increase its return, if the assets in the portfolio have low correlation. MPT has even changed the legal definition of prudence in its impact on the rewriting of the Prudent Investor Rule (now law in most states).

The landmark event in the development of modern portfolio theory was the discovery by Harry Markowitz that diversification – combining assets with low correlation in a portfolio – can **reduce overall risk and increase the portfolio's return**.

His findings were published as "Portfolio Selection" in the *Journal of Finance*, March 1952 (p 77-91). Mean Variance Optimization, the process of analyzing alternative combinations of portfolio assets, with varying returns, risks and correlations, is the statistical innovation that Markowitz brought to investment science. Harry Markowitz, William Sharpe and Merton Miller were awarded the Nobel Prize in Economic Sciences in 1990 for their work in Modern Portfolio Theory.

Modern Portfolio Theory has changed the very definition of prudence. In 1990, in response to overwhelming body of evidence about the unsatisfactory performance of active managers and the benefits of passive asset class investing, the American Law Institute rewrote the Prudent Investor Rule. It has been made into law in most states. It is the law that governs the activities of financial managers.

Modern Portfolio Theory and the Prudent Investor Rule:

> "Economic evidence shows that, from a typical investment perspective, the major capital markets of this country are **highly efficient**, in the sense that available information is rapidly digested and reflected in the market prices of securities.
> As a result, fiduciaries and other investors are confronted with **potent evidence that the application of expertise, investigation and diligence in efforts to 'beat the market'** in these publicly traded securities ordinarily **promises little or no payoff**, or even a **negative payoff** after taking account of research and transaction costs. Empirical research supporting the theory of efficient markets reveals that in such markets skilled professionals have **rarely** been able to identify under-priced securities (that is, to **out guess** the market with respect to future return) with any regularity. In fact, evidence shows that there is **little correlation** between fund managers' earlier successes and their ability to produce above-market returns in subsequent periods."
>
> Reporter's Notes, p 75, The American Law Institute, Restatement of the Law, Trust, Prudent Investor Rule, 1992

That is a pretty strong condemnation of active management – and an equally strong recommendation for Modern Portfolio Theory.

Chapter 19
Investment Statistics Basics

> Abstract - A little bit of statistics (the textbook stuff used by statisticians) is necessary to understand Modern Portfolio Theory. The basics include Standard Deviation (as a measure of volatility – risk), Regression to the Mean, and Normal Distribution (Bell-Curve).

Stock market returns are generally quite random, falling both above and below zero and their averages, but with a very important upward bias. Over a long period of time, returns in a market or a part of a market remain fairly constant. Periods of over- and under-trend performance are often followed by **regression to the mean**. Regression to the mean is a powerful reality in both nature and in investing. It is a technical term of probability and statistics. It means that, left to themselves, things tend to return to normal. The everyday expressions, "things will even out" and "the law of averages" both point at regression to the mean. Since average returns from asset classes tend to be very stable over long periods of time; you should expect periods of higher or lower than average performance to be followed by regression to the mean.

Returns fall around the average in a generally **normal distribution**, the familiar **bell-shaped frequency curve**. Returns fall both above and below the average, with so many more occurrences near the average that the curve bulges up into its bell-shape. The magnitude of the deviations away from the average is descriptive of the risk associated with the investment, and investment managers use the concept of **standard deviation** (a statistical term) to measure it.

The standard deviation tells how far above and below average returns are likely to be over time:

> Returns will be within **One Standard Deviation** of average (either above or below) **68.26%** of the time (7 out of 10 years).
>
> Returns will be within **Two Standard Deviations** of average (either above or below) **95.44%** of the time (19 out of 20 years).
>
> Returns will be within **Three Standard Deviations** of average (either above or below) **99.75%** of the time (199 out of 200 years).

This measure of **volatility** informs us about how often things can, and will, get very weird. A return (or loss) two standard deviations from average is pretty weird, but count on it happening one in twenty years. Three standard deviations almost never happens, but don't count on never; it can, and will, happen about every 200 years (probably not in your lifetime, but who knows, you could get lucky or unlucky).

The important knowledge for investors is that assets that have done very poorly in the recent past are likely to do better in the future. And conversely, assets that have done very well in the recent past are more likely to do poorly in the future. Significant deviations from long term historical averages will likely be "corrected" by regression to the mean (average).

Every investor should be familiar with the concepts of normal distribution, standard deviation and regression to the mean. Ask your financial advisor to explain. If your advisor is not familiar with standard deviation, he (or she) is probably not familiar with modern portfolio theory.

Return and **Volatility** (Standard Deviation) together form the foundation of investment statistical analysis.

A diagram of the actual frequency of the returns of the S&P 500 is remarkably close to the normal distribution predicted by a 20% standard deviation around an 11% average return. The main difference is some 'skew' to the positive side.

The diagram below graphs the number of years with returns within one, two and three standard deviations of average.

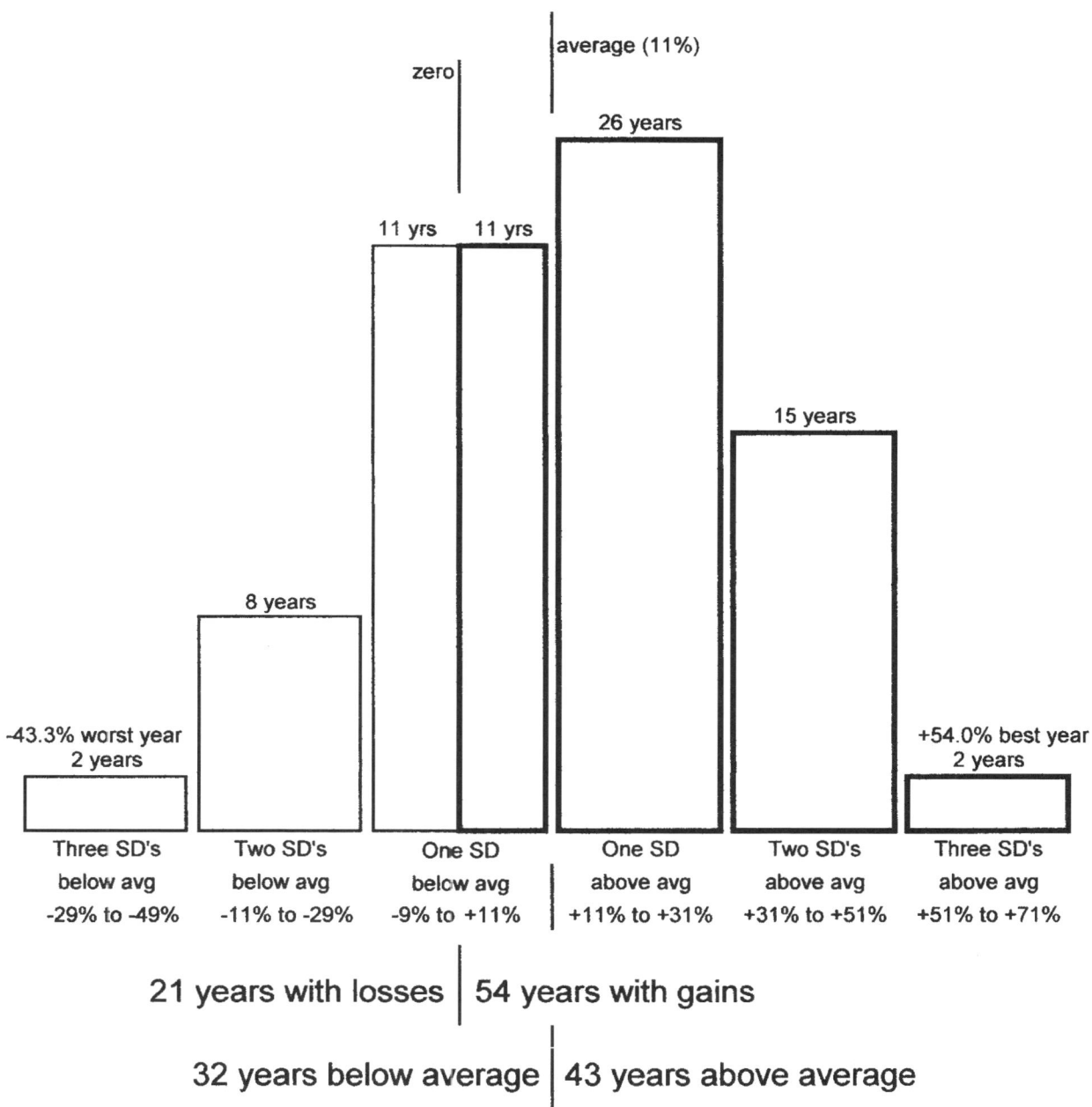

Chapter 20
The Benefits of Low Correlation

Abstract - Low correlation reduces volatility and reduced volatility causes an increase in the compound growth rate (even when the average rate of return is unchanged). Small reductions in volatility compound into significantly increased total returns over time.

Harry Markowitz discovered that you can increase returns over time, by reducing portfolio volatility, even when the average rate of return remains unchanged. Correlation was key.

If two assets move in exact tandem, they have a correlation of +1; if they moved in exactly opposite manner, their correlation would be –1. A portfolio benefits from the addition of assets with less than +1 correlation.

My favorite example comes from Burton Malkiel and involves an island economy with two businesses. One is a resort that does well when it is sunny. The second is an umbrella maker that does well when it rains. The island has a weird climate; it rains half the years, and the sun shines the other half. Each business makes a profit of 50% when it does well and loses 25% when it does badly. Therefore they both have an average return of 12.5% (plus 50% minus 25% divided by 2). If you only own one of the businesses you are stuck with the alternating gains and losses, but you could invest half of your money in each of the two businesses and level out your returns. In any given year one business will lose 25% while the other gains 50% for a net return of 12.5% every year.

TABLE 20.1   ISLAND ECONOMY INVESTMENTS

	A Owning only the resort co.	B Owning only the umbrella co.	C Owning half of each business
Average Annual Return	12.50%	12.50%	12.50%
Volatility (Deviation)	37.50%	37.50%	0%
Compound Growth Rate	5.25%	5.25%	12.50%
Value of $1.00 (20 yrs)	$2.71	$2.71	$9.96

The **compound rate of return** is not the same as the average annual rate of return because of the impact of volatility. In examples A & B, the good and bad years alternate. A $1.00 investment either grows to $1.50 in the first year then shrinks to **$1.125** at the end of the second year; or visa versa, shrinks to $0.75 the first year and then grows to **$1.125** at the end of the second year. In example C, the 12.50% rate of return is constant and the $1.00 grows to $1.125 at the end of the first year and then to **$1.27** at the end of the second year. This apparently small difference after one year really adds up after 20 years. The reduction in volatility in this example increased the compound rate of return from 5.25% to 12.50%; and increases the growth of $1.00 from $2.71 to $9.96.

You can do the same thing with your own portfolio by combining poorly correlated assets. Of course, in the real world there are no perfectly negatively correlated assets. But there are many assets with correlations of less than 1.0 and that's all you need to do to improve your portfolio's performance.

In the following example each portfolio has the same average annual rate of return of 11% (the 75 year average of the S&P 500). The range of standard deviations, from 30% for the speculator (gambler) to 10% for a Modern Portfolio Theory portfolio, is a good representation of the limits that you should expect.

The negative impact of gambling and speculation on long term returns (compound growth rate) can be clearly seen. Even if your winners and losers average out to 11%, if your volatility was high, you would have lost long term return (and gambling and speculation can produce far higher volatility than 30%). Notice especially, the improvement in the compound growth rate of the modern portfolio over the S&P 500 that results from the reduction in volatility.

TABLE 20.2   PORTFOLIO VOLATILITY AND RETURNS

	Speculator/ Gambler		S&P 500 75 yr avg		Modern Portfolio
Average Annual Return	11%	11%	11%	11%	11%
Volatility (Std Deviation)	30%	25%	20%	15%	10%
Compound Growth Rate	7.79%	8.84%	9.65%	10.25%	10.87%
Value of $1.00 (20 yrs)	$4.48	$5.44	$6.31	$7.04	$7.60

Notice the change is the value of $1.00 invested for 20 years. Over time, it really adds up.

Remember, most individuals are earning only a fraction of the S&P 500 return (see Chapter 16); but with higher volatility, their actual nestegg growth is far worse. A diversified modern portfolio is a very important advantage!

Chapter 21
Investment Risk Basics

> Abstract - Diversification is the primary risk management tool of the investor. There are three kinds of investment risk – individual stock risk, stock group risk and market risk. The first two have no return and should be eliminated through diversification. The remaining market risk is almost entirely a short-term phenomenon. In the very long term, portfolio returns can be expected to come very close to its average.

Risk management is largely a matter of controlling portfolio volatility. This is a concept of fundamental importance to investors. Modern Portfolio Theory has made it possible to design portfolios with reduced volatility and higher returns.

There are three kinds of investment risk.

Individual Stock Risk (called specific risk in academia) is the risk associated with any individual company or stock. Having all of your retirement nestegg invested in Enron or GM or any other single stock, is a lot of individual stock risk. Individual stock risk can be virtually eliminated by <u>diversification</u> (most simply by purchasing an asset class index fund).

Stock Group Risk (called extra market risk in academia) is the risk associated with a market sector or business sector. Having all your retirement nestegg invested in energy companies or automotive companies is a lot of stock group risk. Stock group risk can also be virtually eliminated by <u>diversification</u> (again most simply by purchasing an asset class index fund).

Market Risk (called systematic risk in academia) must be managed because it cannot be eliminated.

> *"In an efficient market no incremental reward can or will be earned over the market rate of return by taking either more individual stock risk or more stock group risk"*
> Charles Ellis, The Loser's Game, p 47

There is no **long-term** reward for individual stock risk or stock group risk, both are gambling – period! You can gamble, and sometimes win big, but the house wins in the long run.

> **Diversification is the primary risk management tool for the investor.**

Diversification serves two important risk management purposes in your portfolio:

1. To eliminate individual stock risk and stock group risk, and
2. To reduce volatility (risk) and increase return by adding asset classes that are not highly correlated.

Time changes everything. Risk decreases dramatically with time. The longer your time horizon, the more likely you are to achieve something closer to the "average" return of your portfolio. The short run is a crap shoot.

> *"The stock market is fascinating and very deceptive in the short run. In the very long run, the market is almost boringly reliable"*
> Charles Ellis, The Loser's Game, p 15

Risk is almost entirely a short-term phenomenon! Chapters 22 through 26 outline historical and expected future returns for several important asset classes.

Chapter 22
Investment Return Basics

Abstract - The rates of return for the last 10 and 20 years have been higher than the averages for the last 75 years. Some regression to the mean would argue for somewhat lower returns in the future. Historical returns are outlined.

Some investors have come to expect rates of return that are far in excess of historical averages; many indicated in surveys (around 1998) that they were expecting returns in excess of 20%. I suspect they have adjusted their expectations downward after the last few years of losses for the S&P 500 and NASDAQ. Reasonable expectations are critical to investment and retirement success. What have historical returns really been?

TABLE 22.1   HISTORICAL INVESTMENT RETURNS

75 years from 1926 to 2000	Real Return (Total Return less Inflation)	Total Return
Inflation	0.0%	3.1%
Cash Equivalents, T-Bills, Bank CD's	0.7%	3.8%
Long Term Government Bonds	2.2%	5.3%
Stocks (S&P 500)	7.9%	11.0%
20 years from 1981 to 2000	Real Return (Total Return less Inflation)	Total Return
Inflation	0.0%	5.2%
Cash Equivalents, T-Bills, Bank CD's	1.4%	6.6%
Long Term Government Bonds	6.9%	12.1%
Stocks (S&P 500)	10.5%	15.7%
10 years from 1991 to 2000	Real Return (Total Return less Inflation)	Total Return
Inflation	0.0%	2.6%
Cash Equivalents, T-Bills, Bank CD's	2.1%	4.7%
Long Term Government Bonds	7.8%	10.4%
Stocks (S&P 500)	14.9%	17.5%

Source: DFA

The last 20 (particularly the last 10) years of the 20th century were very good for the investor. Some regression to 75 year mean average is reasonably expectable. Therefore future returns should be expected to be a little lower than the 10 or 20 year returns. The following table provides projected future returns that are probably more reasonable to expect:

TABLE 22.2   PROJECTED FUTURE RETURNS
Slightly lower than the 75 year average (far lower than 10 or 20 year avg)

	Real Return (Total Return less Inflation)	Total Return
Inflation	0.0%	3.0%
Cash Equivalents, T-Bills, Bank CD's	0.5%	3.5%
Long Term Government Bonds	2.5%	5.5%
Stocks (S&P 500)	7.0%	10.0%

Reasonable expectations are crucial for your financial (and mental) health. If you are expecting returns of near 20% in the future you will be (temporarily) comfortable with a smaller annual savings/investment amount. But if returns come in nearer their 75 year average (or lower), you are going to fall far short of your goals. You may then be tempted to make risky 'bets' on some already overpriced high-flyers; and once you start to 'gamble', you risk failing to achieve even average returns.

Several asset classes have been identified by research that have higher returns than the market as a whole.

Chapter 23
Asset Class Research

> Abstract - Several asset classes have been identified by research that have higher returns than the market as a whole. The benefit to your portfolio from adding these is compounded because they not only increase return, but also reduce volatility (risk) because they tend to be poorly correlated with the market as whole (and each other). This is really big news!

Several asset classes based on the Center for Research in Securities Pricing (CRSP) deciles have been the focus of modern portfolio theory research. CRSP divides the entire equities market into ten deciles based on the market capitalization of the New York Stock Exchange. This methodology forms the basis for much more scientific analysis of fund investment style and returns. CRSP deciles allow for precise definitions of market capitalization (large cap, small cap and micro cap).

TABLE 23.1   CRSP DECILES

Decile	Size (millions)	NYSE	AMEX	NASDAQ	TOTAL
1	$511,391	172	5	80	257
2	10,486	172	3	81	256
3	4,428	172	5	136	313
4	2,237	172	5	166	343
5	1,387	172	5	217	394
6	889	172	11	254	437
7	534	172	15	251	438
8	353	172	32	400	604
9	198	172	73	551	796
10	95	172	412	1,399	1,983
Totals		1,720	566	3,535	5,821

The S&P 500 is roughly coterminous with deciles 1 & 2. The Russell 2000 Small Cap Index covers approximately deciles 5-8. Deciles 9 & 10 are micro cap. The Wilshire 5000 covers the whole market (it used to be closer to 5000 stocks, now it's more).

CRSP uses a similar decile system to analyze book-to-market value, creating in effect a 10 x 10 style box. This is a substantial improvement over the more anecdotal Morningstar style boxes, which has only 9 boxes of texture to define the market.

While the Morningstar style boxes are an important innovation, they provide limited and sometimes misleading information. For instance, both a Russell 2000 and a CRSP 9-10 fund would be called "small cap" in the Morningstar system. The micro cap stocks, and their return premium, are obfuscated. Regarding value, most retail value funds hold stocks in the bottom half of book-to-market value that dilutes the lowest deciles of value. DFA value funds, based on CRSP size and value deciles, hold stocks only in the bottom 10% of value for large cap stocks and the bottom 25% for small cap stocks. All small is not the same; all value is not the same.

CRSP Deciles

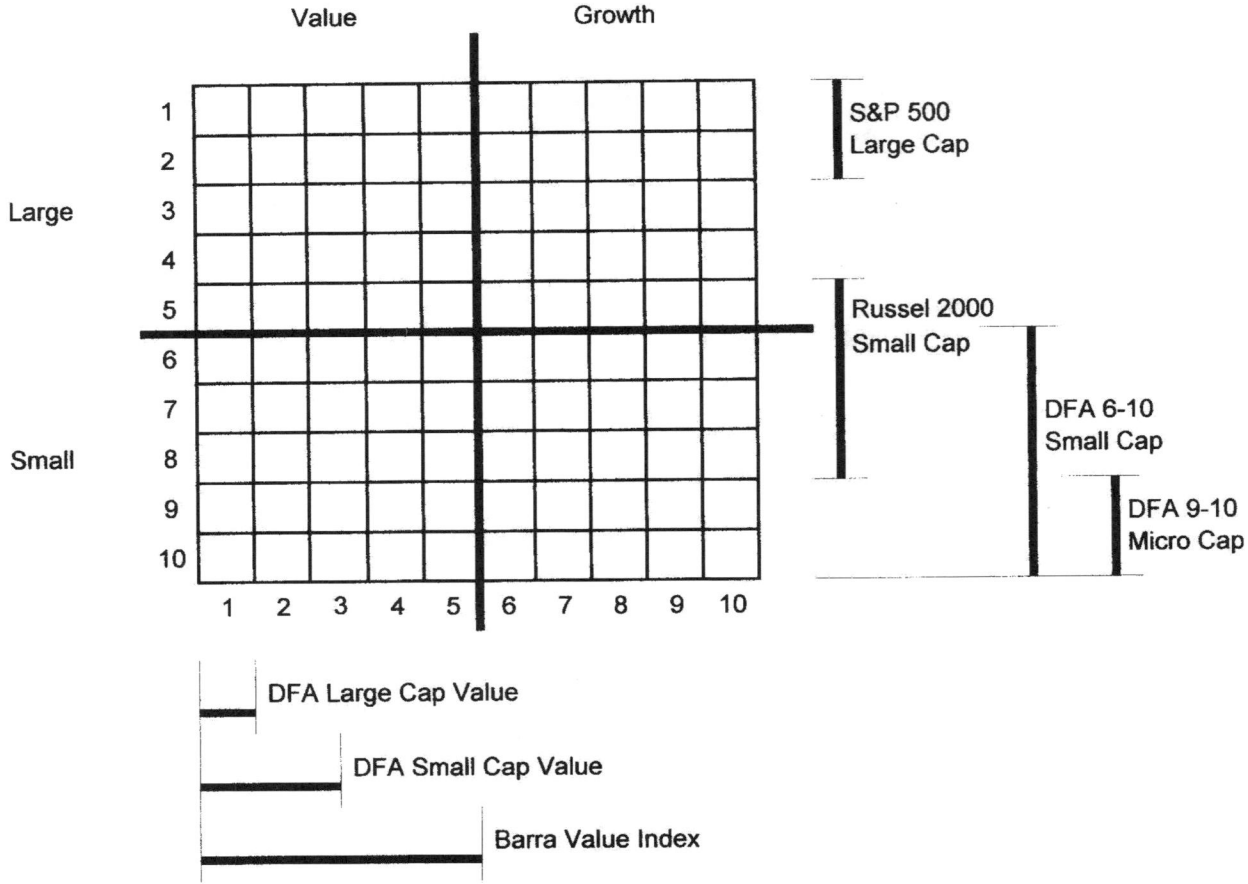

Morningstar Style Boxes

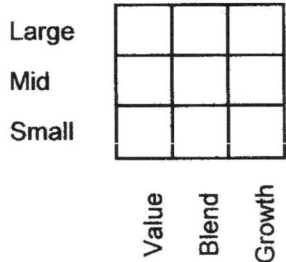

The following table contains data on wide range of asset classes, including small and value.

TABLE 23.2   HISTORICAL ASSET CLASS RETURNS

75 years from 1926 to 2000	Real Return (Total Return less Inflation)	Total Return	Growth of $1,000
Inflation	0.0%	3.1%	$9,872
Cash Equivalents, T-Bills, Bank CD's	0.7%	3.8%	16,398
Long Term Government Bonds	2.2%	5.3%	48,098
Large Cap (deciles 1-2, S&P 500)	7.9%	11.0%	2,507,399
Small Cap (deciles 6-10)	8.8%	11.9%	4,594,693
Micro Cap (deciles 9-10)	9.6%	12.7%	7,839,596
Large Cap (deciles 1-5) **Value**	9.8%	12.9%	8,954,589
Small Cap (deciles 6-10) **Value**	11.7%	14.8%	31,307,011
20 years from 1981 to 2000	Real Return (Total Return less Inflation)	Total Return	Growth of $1,000
Inflation	0.0%	5.2%	$2,756
Cash Equivalents, T-Bills, Bank CD's	1.4%	6.6%	3,590
Long Term Government Bonds	6.9%	12.1%	9,820
Large Cap (deciles 1-2, S&P 500)	10.5%	15.7%	18,479
Small Cap (deciles 6-10)	8.5%	13.7%	13,038
Micro Cap (deciles 9-10)	7.9%	13.1%	11,729
Large Cap (deciles 1-5) **Value**	11.4%	16.6%	21,576
Small Cap (deciles 6-10) **Value**	12.4%	17.6%	25,594
10 years from 1991 to 2000	Real Return (Total Return less Inflation)	Total Return	Growth of $1,000
Inflation		2.6%	$1,293
Cash Equivalents, T-Bills, Bank CD's	2.1%	4.7%	1,583
Long Term Government Bonds	7.8%	10.4%	2,690
Large Cap (deciles 1-2, S&P 500)	14.9%	17.5%	5,016
Small Cap (deciles 6-10)	15.1%	17.7%	5,102
Micro Cap (deciles 9-10)	17.5%	20.1%	6,244
Large Cap (deciles 1-5) **Value**	15.7%	18.3%	5,368
Small Cap (deciles 6-10) **Value**	17.3%	19.9%	6,140

Source: DFA

Since asset class returns have been strong in the last 10 and 20 years, some regression to the mean is likely. Projected future returns indicate a continuing premium for **small** (and **micro**) cap and for **value**.

TABLE 23.3   PROJECTED FUTURE RETURNS
Slightly lower than the 75 year average (far lower than 10 or 20 year avg)

	Real Return (Total Return less Inflation)	Total Return
Inflation	0.0%	3.0%
Cash Equivalents, T-Bills, Bank CD's	0.5%	3.5%
Long Term Government Bonds	2.5%	5.5%
Large Cap (deciles 1-2, S&P 500)	7.0%	10.0%
Small Cap (deciles 6-10)	8.0%	11.0%
Micro Cap (deciles 9-10)	9.0%	12.0%
Large Cap (deciles 1-5) **Value**	9.0%	12.0%
Small Cap (deciles 6-10) **Value**	11.0%	14.0%

In the next chapter we will look at the research on small and value stocks.

Chapter 24
Small Cap and Value Stock Investing
The Three Factor Model

> Abstract - Two broad asset classes in particular – small cap and value – have been identified as providing higher return than the market as a whole. Small cap investments clearly have more risk (volatility), but value investments seem to have lower risk.

According to the research of Eugene Fama and Kenneth French, three factors explain most of portfolio returns: market, size and value exposure. In "The Cross Section of Expected Stock Returns", *Journal of Finance*, June 1992, (p 427-465) using CRSP data they analyzed returns from 1964-1992. They concluded that the combination of exposure to the market (market return) plus exposure to small cap stocks (size) plus exposure to high book-to-market value stocks (value) explains 95% of the variability of returns.

In short, the bottom 3 deciles of size, showed a 5% premium over the top 3 deciles; and the deepest 3 deciles of book-to-market value showed a 5% premium over the 3 highest growth deciles.

Size Effect

The original research on the size effect was performed by Rolf Banz. He found in 1981 that returns increase with decreases in size as measured by market capitalization.

> Rolf Banz, The Relationship Between Return and Market Value of Common Stocks, Journal of Financial Economics, Mar 1981, p 3-18

Small company stocks carry greater risk (and therefore have higher returns) because they have more limited resources and their earnings are more variable. The don't have the deep pockets to easily survive market turmoil (especially when deep and prolonged).

Fama and French have published more recent research that confirms a smaller (but still positive) size premium and a continuing strong value premium.

> James L. Davis, Eugene F. Fama and Kenneth R. French, Characteristics, Covariances, and Average Returns: 1927-1997 CRSP Working Paper #471

There have been many nay-sayers about the small cap effect in recent years. The recent superior performance of large cap stocks from 1995 to 1998 with the S&P 500 averaging over 30% return and small caps only about 15% has fueled the discussion. Since then, small caps have outperformed large caps again. This is the nature of the beast. Short term results will always be surprising; it's the long term that counts.

Value Effect

Value investing involves companies that are not currently doing well. These "distressed" companies are those trading closest to their "liquidation" value. Companies with a high book-to-market value are risky companies.

It turns out that these **risky** companies make **great** investments (while great companies may not) – counterintuitive!

Michele Clayman studied and compared excellent and unexcellent companies in her research of value investing. She published "In search of Excellence: The Investor's Viewpoint", *Financial Analysts Journal*, June 1987, p 63; and "Excellence Revisited", *Financial Analysts Journal*, May-June 1994, p 61-65. She found that, as investments, "unexcellent" companies significantly outperformed "excellent" companies.

This does not mean that "unexcellent" companies outperformed "excellent" companies, as companies; they did not. But "unexcellent" companies were better investments. For the period 1981-1985 she found the following:

TABLE 24.1   UNEXCELLENT AND EXCELLENT COMPANIES

	Unexcellent Companies	Excellent Companies
Asset Growth	5.93%	21.78%
Equity Growth	3.76%	18.43%
Return on Total Capital	4.88%	16.04%
Return on Equity	7.09%	19.05%
Return on Sales	2.49%	8.62%
Return on $100 Investment	$297.50	$181.60

Unexcellent companies – great investments!

In his 1996 letter to clients studied 1976-1996, Michael Berry of Heartland Advisors found that value stocks have not only outperformed growth stocks over the long term, they also had lower standard deviation, providing important protection, particularly in bear markets.

TABLE 24.2   VALUE RETURNS AND STANDARD DEVIATION

	VALUE		GROWTH	
	Return	Std Dev	Return	Std Dev
Small Cap	20.4%	5.1%	18.0%	6.4%
Mid Cap	18.0%	4.5%	16.7%	5.9%
Large Cap	15.9%	3.8%	12.1%	4.9%

Increased return, lower risk – this is about as close to the free lunch we are going to get!

> *"The best available data would indicate that a strong tilt to value and a higher representation of small company stocks in equity portfolios will handsomely reward long-term investors"*
>
> Frank Armstrong, Investment Advisor

Chapter 25
Fixed Income Investing

Abstract - Fixed income securities will reduce the volatility of your portfolio. Conventional wisdom argues for 40% to 50% fixed income in a "conservative" portfolio. Those including that much are paying a very high price in long term returns. Rule of thumb: no more than 10% fixed income for accumulation phase, 25% fixed income in early retirement, and 50% fixed income in very late retirement. Short-term bonds have less volatility and lower correlation to equities than long-term bonds. Bonds with maturities over 5 years don't offer sufficient reward for their higher risk.

Fixed income securities should be included in most, if not all, individual investors' portfolios. But the addition of fixed income to a portfolio reduces **long-term** returns.

The extreme variability of short-term returns causes many investors to include from 40% to 50% fixed income in their portfolios. Conventional wisdom argues for 40% to 50% fixed income in a "conservative" portfolio. But those including that much are paying a very high price in long-term returns. Remember, risk is almost entirely a short-term phenomenon; so the question about fixed income allocation is all about time horizons.

Those investors with very long-term time horizons, like young persons beginning to accumulate their nesteggs, will benefit from staying closer to 10%; but it will be a wild ride. Those with somewhat shorter time horizons, like those nearing or in early retirement, may want to include something closer to 25% to 30% in fixed income, to provide cash reserves and better sleep. Time horizons in retirement of 20, 30 or more years are not all that short and the penalty in decreased returns is too severe to argue for 40% or 50% fixed income for most retirees. Only those with very short time horizons of 5, 10 or under 20 years should consider fixed income percentages of 40%, 50% or higher.

Research has shown that short-term bonds have less volatility (than long-term bonds) and lower correlation to equities.

Eugene Fama in "Time Varying Expected Returns" (Feb 1988, unpublished paper, data updated regularly) studies the returns of bonds. He finds that the time premium for longer term bonds is not reliable; that is, long term bonds have widely variable rates of return. He also finds that bonds with maturities beyond five years don't offer sufficient reward for their higher risk.

David Plecha (DFA) has confirmed the poor return/risk characteristics of long term bonds in his March 1997 Working Paper "Fixed Income Investing". For the period 1964-1996 Plecha found that increase in yields from increasing maturity breaks down beyond five years maturity.

TABLE 25.1   FIXED INCOME RETURNS AND STANDARD DEVIATION

	Return	Standard Deviation
1 month T-Bill	6.49%	1.28%
1 year T-Bill	7.46%	2.10%
5 year Note	7.77%	6.58%
Long-Term Bonds	7.32%	11.48%

Maturities for all fixed income securities should therefore be kept to under five years.

Chapter 26
International Investing

> Abstract - International equities should be included in a modern portfolio because of their low correlation to U.S. markets. Emerging markets have particularly low correlation.

In 1970 the international equity market was only about 30% of total world equities; today it is about 60%. Although the U.S. market has increased since 1970, it has not increased nearly as fast as the international market.

Returns for the period 1970-2000 have been

TABLE 26.1 INTERNATIONAL RETURNS (1970-2000)

	Total Return
International Large	14.1%
International Small	15.3%
International Large **Value** *(1975-2000)*	18.7%
International Small **Value**	15.3%
Emerging Markets *(1985-2000)*	9.2%

Frank Armstrong, The Informed Investor

While returns from 1970-2000 from international equities have been better than from U.S. equities, their importance for portfolio mix is from their low correlation to U.S. markets. Emerging markets have particularly low correlation with the U.S.

> *"Just as investors a decade ago were overly optimistic about foreign diversification, investors today are overly pessimistic about it. Foreign stocks belong in every portfolio."*
>
> William Berstein
> The Intelligent Asset Allocator, p 50

The last 30 years have been good for international equities. Some regression is reasonably expectable. Therefore future returns should be expected to be a little lower than the recent past. The following table provides projected future returns that are probably more reasonable to expect:

TABLE 26.2 PROJECTED FUTURE INTERNATIONAL RETURNS
Slightly lower than the 30 year average

	Total Return
International Large	12.0%
International Small	13.0%
International Large **Value**	14.0%
International Small **Value**	15.0%
Emerging Markets	12.0%

Attractive returns, low correlation – very important to your portfolio.

Chapter 27
Real Estate Asset Class Investing

Abstract - Real estate assets tend to have low correlation with equities. But REIT's are not quite as poorly correlated and throw off a lot of taxable income. REIT's should therefore be held only in tax-deferred accounts (if at all).

Real Estate assets tend to perform well in periods of high inflation, when the replacement cost of real estate is driven up. Inflation, at the same time, tends to drive down the price of stocks and bonds. Bonds tend to do poorly in inflation, but they provide great protection and performance during periods of deflation.

Real estate assets tend to have very low correlations with equities in general. Although Real Estate Investment Trusts (REIT's) are not quite as poorly correlated with stocks as the real estate assets themselves, they still offer some diversification and protection. REIT's seem in particular to have a relatively high correlation with the small cap asset class. Because of this, many have concluded that they have more in common with stocks than with real estate itself (which is not highly correlated with stocks).

Even so, REIT's may be able to provide some additional diversification in a modern portfolio. If you choose to include real estate in your portfolio, you need to protect yourself from its poor tax performance. Because most of the return from REIT's is from dividends, they are taxable at your full marginal rate rather than as capital gains. If you own REIT's, hold them only in tax-deferred accounts.

Part Four

Modern Portfolio Management

Chapter 28
Asset Allocation

> Abstract - There are five basic components of asset allocation: fixed income, value, small cap, international, and emerging markets.

There are endless portfolio alternatives and they can be explored in mind numbing precision by Mean Variance Optimization and Monte Carlo software (which I own and confess to playing with). In the end you must determine your own goals, objectives and tolerance for risk in order to build an appropriate portfolio. The main decisions are the following:

A. How much fixed income?

The spectrum normally runs from 10% to 50% of the total portfolio. Very few will reasonably fall outside this range. 10% for accumulators; 25% for retirees with long time horizons; and up to 50% for retirees with short time horizons is a good place to start.

B. How much value?

The spectrum again normally runs from 25% to 50% of equities. The value premium (expected higher returns) appears quite strong, and the risk (volatility) appears quite low. For these reasons, a 50% allocation of all your equities to value (including large and small value) is a good place to start, adding to long term return and reducing risk (volatility).

C. How much small cap?

The spectrum normally runs from 25% to 50% of equities. Even though it will add some volatility, a 50% allocation of all your equities to small cap (including small value) will add long term return and provide significant diversification.

D. How much international?

The spectrum normally runs from 10% to 40% of equities. Given that the rest of the world will have a higher rate of growth than the U.S., a large allocation of your equities to international may be very important in the long term. In addition, a large international allocation guards against the negative impact of the probable continuing depreciation of the dollar and provides a volatility damper from its low correlation with the U.S. A 30% to 40% international allocation is a good place to start.

E. How much emerging markets?

The spectrum normally runs from 5% to 20% of your international equities. For the same reasons as for international equities (and small and value assets), generally a 20% emerging market allocation (of international equities) appears to be a good long term strategy.

The modern portfolios which follow are all based on a **4 x 25%** approach for US equities (25% each of large cap, large cap value, small cap and small cap value) and a **5 x 20%** approach for international equities (20% each of large cap, large cap value, small cap, small cap value and emerging markets).

There are endless model portfolios, endless potential mean optimization analyses, and endless personality and risk tolerance profiling available to you. You can avail yourself of as much or as little of it as you want. But the most important thing you can do is be disciplined when weird stuff happens in the future. The actual choice of specific portfolio is far less important than your ability to buy it and then hold it!

In addition, the Mean Variance Optimization process itself is particularly vulnerable to data manipulation, in that very small changes in input data can dramatically change its output. For each asset class we must enter an expected rate of return, a standard deviation (risk), and a correlation to every other asset class.

The potential for distortions from over analysis is so significant that William Bernstein is cautioning against its use to develop detailed portfolio alternatives. He comments that "naive" portfolios can be expected to beat active management, and the most important component of investor success is investor behavior – a long-term buy-and-hold discipline.

Once you decide on the asset classes you want to hold in your portfolio, you should be careful to hold tax inefficient funds in tax-deferred accounts to the maximum extent possible.

The following table provides some general guidance about where some asset classes should be held.

TABLE 28.1   ASSETS CLASSES FOR TAXABLE VS TAX-DEFERRED ACCOUNTS

Asset Class	Tax-Deferred	Taxable
Fixed Income	best in tax deferred accounts	ok
Equities		
U.S. Large Cap	ok	ok
U.S Large Cap Value	best in tax deferred accounts	ok (TM better)
U.S. Small Cap	best in tax deferred accounts	ok (TM better)
U.S. Micro Cap	ok	poor
U.S. Small Cap Value	best in tax deferred accounts	ok (TM better)
Int'l Large Cap	ok	ok
Int'l Large Cap Value	best in tax deferred accounts	ok (TM better)
Int'l Small Cap	best in tax deferred accounts	ok (TM better)
Int'l Small Cap Value	ok	poor
Emerging Markets	best in tax deferred accounts	ok
REIT's	only ok in tax deferred accounts	poor

TM = Tax Managed Index Fund

Every situation is different. Some of us have mostly taxable accounts. Most of us have quite a bit in tax deferred accounts. Holding tax inefficient funds (like U.S. micro cap) in taxable accounts is not the end of the world. It's just not best, if it can be avoided.

The following chapters offer some starting points for a portfolio.

Chapter 29
The Modern Power Portfolio

Abtract - The Modern Power Portfolio provides a portfolio of DFA funds. DFA has designed a whole family of index funds based on the Nobel Prize winning strategies of Modern Portfolio Theory. To gain access to these funds, individuals must retain the services of an independent financial advisor approved by DFA.

Dimensional Fund Advisors (DFA) was founded in 1981 offering modern portfolio theory index funds to institutional investors. DFA now offers over 30 low cost asset class index funds based on the research we have just reviewed. These funds are available to individuals only through financial advisors. A limited group of financial advisors has been approved by DFA. Each must demonstrate a commitment to buy-and-hold passive asset class index fund investing. Their fees are an additional cost to individual DFA investors. Whether it makes sense to pay these fees to gain access to DFA is the subject of some debate. Fees range from flat fees of from $1,200 to $2,000 to percentage fees of 0.5% to 1.25% of assets under management. DFA funds have a minimum investment of $3,000.

TABLE 29.1 THE MODERN POWER PORTFOLIO

	DFA Funds for **Tax-Deferred Accounts**	DFA Funds for **Taxable Accounts**		Allocations		
Money Mkt		VMMXX Money Mkt *(six months of average expenses)*				
Fixed Income	*(percent of **total portfolio**)*			10%	25%	40%
One Yr U.S.	DFIHX One Yr Fixed	DFIHX One Yr Fixed	33.3%	of fixed income		
Five Yr U.S.	DFFGX Five Yr Gov't	DFFGX Five Yr Gov't	33.3%	of fixed income		
Five Yr Global	DFGBX Five Yr Global	DFGBX Five Yr Global	33.3%	of fixed income		
Equities	*(percent of **total portfolio**)*			90%	75%	60%
U.S. Equities	*(percent of **equities**)*			60%	65%	70%
Lg Cap	DFLCX Large Cap	DFLCX Large Cap	25%	of US Equities		
Lg Cap Value	DFLVX Lg Value	DTMMX **TM** Mktwide Value	25%	of US Equities		
Sm Cap	DFSTX Small Cap	DFTSX **TM** Small Cap	25%	of US Equities		
Micro Cap	DFSCX Micro Cap *(from small cap allocation if used)*					
Sm Cap Value	DFSVX Sm Cap Value	DTMVX **TM** Small Value	25%	of US Equities		
Int'l Equities	*(percent of **equities**)*			40%	35%	30%
Lg Cap	DFALX Int'l Large	DFALX Int'l Large	20%	of Int'l Equities		
Lg Cap Value	DFIVX Int'l Value	DTMIX **TM** Int'l Value	20%	of Int'l Equities		
Sm Cap	DFISX Int'l Small	DFISX Int'l Small	20%	of Int'l Equities		
Sm Cap Value	DISVX Int'l Small Value	DISVX Int'l Small Value	20%	of Int'l Equities		
Emerging Mkts	DFEMX Emerging Mkts	DFEMX Emerging Mkts	20%	of Int'l Equities		

The Modern Power Portfolio above uses DFA funds to reach into the 9th and 10th deciles of small cap and into deep value. If the research is right, there is a little extra return available for having accomplished this. These portfolios are based on the 4 x 25% US and 5 x 20% International asset allocations outlined in the previous chapter.

The portfolios above are all DFA funds except for the money market account. When you set up your DFA account you will be establishing a institutional custodial account with Charles Schwab or some other broker, which will automatically contain their money market account. I use a Vanguard (VMMXX) Prime Money Market account in addition because it pays about 0.5% more interest than Schwab's. You can confirm whether it's worth it for you.

The following table contains historical and projected returns data for the Modern Power Portfolios in Table 29.1.

TABLE 29.2   DFA MODERN POWER PORTFOLIO RETURNS DATA

	Fixed Income %			Fixed Income Percentage		
				10%	25%	40%
		NASDAQ	S&P 500			
Actual Returns	1992	15.46%	7.42%	8.03%	8.96%	9.40%
	1993	14.75%	9.89%	23.80%	20.45%	17.39%
	1994	-3.20%	1.18%	3.11%	1.94%	0.92%
	1995	39.92%	37.45%	21.66%	20.98%	19.88%
	1996	22.71%	22.88%	14.04%	13.55%	12.83%
	1997	21.64%	33.19%	11.74%	12.49%	12.62%
	1998	39.63%	28.62%	6.96%	6.86%	6.76%
	1999	85.59%	21.07%	20.68%	17.35%	14.24%
	2000	-39.29%	-9.06%	-1.79%	-0.11%	1.81%
	2001	-21.05%	-12.02%	0.81%	2.45%	3.80%
Growth of $1,000 (over 2 years)		$479	$800	$990	$1,023	$1,057
Growth of $1,000 (over 3 years)		$890	$969	$1,195	$1,204	$1,207
Growth of $1,000 (over 10 years)		$3,327	$3,348	$2,732	$2,659	$2,544
Expected Long Term Return			10.0%	11.8%	11.0%	10.2%
Expected Standard Deviation			20.0%	12.5%	11.5%	9.5%

You can see that the Modern Portfolio is weakly correlated with the S&P 500. Sometimes the S&P 500 outperforms (1995–1998). Sometimes the Modern Portfolio outperforms (1993, 2000 and 2001). Sometimes they are fairly similar (1992, 1994, 1999).

The NASDAQ has been far more volatile and those that chased the extraordinary results of 1999 rode the NASDAQ back down through its recent collapse.

You can also see the impact of adding fixed income. Some years it helped returns (1993, 1997, 2000, 2001). Some years it hurt returns (1993-1996, 1999). Some years it made very little difference (like 1998).

As the last three years have indicated, a Modern Portfolio is a safer long-term investment.

You can contact DFA directly at www.dfafunds.com to find approved advisors in your area. I am currently using Evanson Asset Management because Steven Evanson uses a flat fee approach for all passive asset class investing clients. His fees range from $1,200 to $2,000 per year no matter how large your portfolio becomes (he can be contacted at www.evansonasset.com).

Chapter 30
The Do-it-yourself Modern Portfolio

Abstract - If you want to go it alone, and avoid all these advisor fees, Vanguard offers a family of funds that will allow you to take advantage of good (though not as excellent as DFA) diversification into small cap, value and international equities and short-term bonds.

The growth of retail index funds in the last few years has greatly expanded the available alternatives. It is now possible to construct a perfectly good passive asset class index fund portfolio entirely from Vanguard (or several other families of funds).

TABLE 30.1   THE DO-IT-YOURSELF MODERN PORTFOLIO

		Vanguard Funds for **Tax-Deferred Accounts**		Vanguard Funds for **Taxable Accounts**			Allocations	
Money Mkt				VMMXX Money Mkt six months of average expenses				
Fixed Income		(percent of **total portfolio**)				10%	25%	40%
Sht Term Bonds	VBISX	Sht Term Bond Index	VBISX	Sht Term Bond Index		100%	of fixed income	
Equities		(percent of **total portfolio**)				90%	75%	60%
U.S. Equities		(percent of **equities**)				**60%**	**65%**	**70%**
Lg Cap	VFINX	S&P 500 Index	VTGIX	**TM** G&I (S&P 500)		25%	of US Equities	
Lg Cap Value	VIVAX	Value Index	VIVAX	Value Index		25%	of US Equities	
Sm Cap	NAESX	Small Cap	VTMSX	**TM** Small Cap		25%	of US Equities	
Micro Cap		no Vanguard micro cap index fund						
Sm Cap Value	VISVX	Small Cap Value	VISVX	Small Cap Value		25%	of US Equities	
Int'l Equities		(percent of **equities**)				**40%**	**35%**	**30%**
Lg Cap	VGTSX	Total Int'l Index	VTMGX	**TM** International		75%	of Int'l Equities	
Lg Cap Value	VTRIX	Int'l Value	VTRIX	Int'l Value		25%	of Int'l Equities	
Sm Cap		no Vanguard small cap Int'l funds						
Sm Cap Value		no Vanguard small cap value Int'l funds						
Emerging Mkts		included in VGTSX and VTMGX						

You can immediately see that Vanguard lacks some of the depth that DFA offers. Vanguard's weaknesses are: small cap misses deciles 9-10; less deep value exposure than DFA; no international small cap or small cap value; fewer tax-managed alternatives for taxable accounts. Vanguard funds have a minimum investment of at least $1,000 each (the tax-managed funds require $3,000).

While not as powerful as the DFA based Modern Power Portfolio, this is a very good alternative for most investors. It can be expected to outperform all but a very small handful of active managers. Because of its exposure to small cap and value equities and diversification into international and emerging markets, it can be expected to have somewhat higher returns and lower volatility than the market as a whole.

The following table contains historical and projected returns data for the portfolios in table 30.1.

TABLE 30.2   DO-IT-YOURSELF MODERN PORTFOLIO RETURNS DATA

				Fixed Income Percentage		
Fixed Income %				10%	25%	40%
		NASDAQ	S&P 500			
Actual Returns	1992	15.46%	7.42%	4.79%	6.35%	7.32%
	1993	14.75%	9.89%	21.24%	18.58%	16.15%
	1994	-3.20%	1.18%	2.28%	1.26%	0.35%
	1995	39.92%	37.45%	23.56%	22.65%	21.39%
	1996	22.71%	22.88%	14.19%	13.09%	11.79%
	1997	21.64%	33.19%	15.77%	15.47%	14.71%
	1998	39.63%	28.62%	13.03%	11.94%	10.93%
	1999	85.59%	21.07%	18.39%	15.19%	12.18%
	2000	-39.29%	-9.06%	-1.80%	0.56%	2.84%
	2001	-21.05%	-12.02%	-6.81%	-3.58%	-0.61%
Growth of $1,000 (over 2 years)		$479	$800	$915	$970	$1,022
Growth of $1,000 (over 3 years)		$890	$969	$1,083	$1,118	$1,147
Growth of $1,000 (over 10 years)		$3,327	$3,348	$2,604	$2,560	$2,477
Expected Long Term Return				10.0%	11.4%	10.4%	9.4%
Expected Standard Deviation				20.0%	13.0%	12.0%	10.0%

You can contact Vanguard directly at www.vanguard.com or 800-831-9996 to obtain information about their funds. You should be careful to look for new funds that fill in their weaknesses in the future.

Chapter 31
The Simplified Modern Portfolio

Abstract - The Simplified Modern Portfolio described here (containing as few as 4 mutual funds) would have outperformed all but a very small handful of active managers (and who knows who's going to be hot – next year?).

The **"Simplified Modern Portfolio"** is a very simple passive index strategy that is a very powerful alternative that will work for most people. The "Simplified Modern Portfolio" includes as few as only four mutual funds:

TABLE 31.1 THE SIMPLIFIED MODERN PORTFOLIO

	Vanguard Funds for **Tax-Deferred Accounts**		Vanguard Funds for **Taxable Accounts**			Allocations	
Money Mkt			VMMXX Money Mkt six months of average expenses				
Fixed Income	(percent of **total portfolio**)				10%	25%	40%
Sht Term Bonds	VBISX	Sht Term Bond Index	VBISX	Sht Term Bond Index	100%	of fixed income	
Equities	(percent of **total portfolio**)				90%	75%	60%
U.S. Equities	(percent of **equities**)				60%	65%	70%
Lg Cap	VFINX	S&P 500 Index	VTGIX	**TM** G&I (S&P 500)	50%	of US Equities	
Sm Cap Value	VISVX	Small Cap Value	VISVX	Small Cap Value	50%	of US Equities	
Int'l Equities	(percent of **equities**)				40%	35%	30%
Lg Cap	VGTSX	Total Int'l Index	VTMGX	**TM** International	100%	of Int'l Equities	

These funds have a minimum investment of at least $1,000 each (the tax-managed funds require $3,000). If you have only two thousand to start with, divide it between the bond fund and large cap. Next year add small cap, then international. Once you have all of asset classes covered you can begin to spread your investment to create the detailed allocation percentages you have established. At that point, all that's left is to rebalance once a year.

This very simple portfolio, consisting of only four funds, would have outperformed all but a small handful of the active managers over the last 20 years (and who knows who's going to be hot – next year).

TABLE 31.2 SIMPLIFIED MODERN PORTFOLIO RETURNS DATA

		NASDAQ	S&P 500	Fixed Income 10%	Fixed Income 25%	Fixed Income 40%
Actual Returns	1992	15.46%	7.42%	3.22%	4.82%	6.04%
	1993	14.75%	9.89%	20.27%	17.67%	15.34%
	1994	-3.20%	1.18%	2.75%	1.64%	0.65%
	1995	39.92%	37.45%	24.31%	23.31%	21.94%
	1996	22.71%	22.88%	14.22%	13.18%	11.91%
	1997	21.64%	33.19%	16.86%	16.39%	15.46%
	1998	39.63%	28.62%	15.73%	14.44%	13.13%
	1999	85.59%	21.07%	17.63%	14.38%	11.39%
	2000	-39.29%	-9.06%	-1.26%	1.26%	3.46%
	2001	-21.05%	-12.02%	-5.96%	-2.72%	0.20%
Growth of $1,000 (over 2 years)		$479	$800	$929	$985	$1,037
Growth of $1,000 (over 3 years)		$890	$969	$1,092	$1,127	$1,155
Growth of $1,000 (over 10 years)		$3,327	$3,348	$2,675	$2,626	$2,534
Expected Long Term Return			10.0%	11.1%	10.1%	9.2%
Expected Standard Deviation			20.0%	13.5%	12.5%	10.5%

If you adopt this strategy you will have avoided the biggest problem encountered by most investors – losing money.

> *"Even though most investors see their work as active, assertive and on the offensive, the reality is, and should be, that stock and bond investing alike are primarily a defensive process. The great secret for success in long term investing is to avoid serious losses."*
>
> Charles Ellis, The Loser's Game, p 56

Chapter 32
Making the Most of Your Plan's Funds

Abstract - The strategy outlined below will allow you to apply the principles of Modern Portfolio Theory to the limited number of funds available in your company retirement plan.

If your company's retirement plan limits you to a small group of funds you must select from, you can still put together a modern portfolio. The steps below will help you sort through the funds available to you.

Your first task is always to select the asset classes you want to hold in your portfolio (Chapter 28). You should always look for index funds, or funds with the lowest expenses.

Step One: Find a short term bond fund. You are looking for average and maturity of from two to five years, but seven years is okay. Choose an index fund if it is available.

Step Two: Find a large cap fund (preferably an S&P 500 index fund).

You will be able to complete steps one and two in almost every family of funds. If you can go no further, don't be too disappointed. A simple mix of short term bonds and large cap stocks is still a very good portfolio. If you can go on to step three below you will improve your diversification (improving returns and reducing risk).

Step Three: Try to find small cap, value, small-cap value and international asset class funds.

Most of you will find at least one of these four asset classes. Some will find two, or three, or even all four. Depending on how many "step three" funds you have available, you can use one of the portfolios from the preceding Chapters as a pattern for your portfolio allocation.

Chapter 33
Working with a Financial Advisor

> Abstract - Work only with a fee-only-advisor who understands Modern Portfolio Theory and commit your investment policy to writing.

How can you get good, unbiased advice? The answer is really fairly simple. **First**, use a fee-only-advisor. **Second**, assure yourself that your advisor understands Modern Portfolio Theory. **Third**, commit your investment policy to writing.

Fee-only-advisor. Work only with financial advisors who earn their income from their advice and financial planning services. Do not work with commission-based advisors (they have a natural bias toward investment products and strategies that earn them commissions rather than earn returns for you). This conflict of interest is unnecessary – find a fee-only-advisor. Even with a fee-only-advisor, always be clear about any additional commissions on the "products" they are recommending to you. Ask explicitly.

You can expect fees to range from 0.5% to 1.25% of your nestegg (assets under management) per year. If your nestegg is less than $500,000 you will be at the high end of the range. If your nestegg is over $1,000,000 you should be able to negotiate a fee toward the low end of the range. Some advisors, such as Evanson Asset Management, offer a very low flat annual fee for Modern Portfolio management (recognizing the limited management required for passive asset class investing).

You should always use a large well-known brokerage firm, such as Fidelity, Schwab, Vanguard, TD Waterhouse or Jack White, to hold your nestegg assets. Be sure that their statements are mailed directly to you. You will need to execute a limited power of attorney to allow your advisor to trade on your account. Be sure it does not allow your advisor the right to withdraw funds from your account.

Modern Portfolio Theory. Confirm that your advisor understands Modern Portfolio Theory and is committed to its tenets. Be aware that many advisors claim to believe in Modern Portfolio Theory but are still involved in active management. If your advisor is recommending individual stocks, trying to time exposure to and withdrawal from the market, or chasing recent high performance by funds or money managers, he is practicing active management. If he believes that you can regularly beat the benchmarks, he is not convinced that the market is efficient. Trying to "beat the benchmark" should be a warning to you. The evidence has shown that funds and managers do not succeed over long periods, and tend not to repeat even from year to year. You want to track the benchmark, not beat it.

If a fund or manager appears to have beaten a benchmark for several years, ask about the benchmark. Comparing a manager to the wrong benchmark could make him look like the next Warren Buffet. Ask to see a value manager compared to an appropriate value benchmark. Compare each fund or money manager to the most appropriate available benchmark.

Investment Policy. Commit your investment policy to writing with your financial advisor (See Chapter 35). Your advisor can help you clarify your goals and objectives, time horizon, risk tolerance, and asset allocation. The most important thing your advisor can do is help you stay the course when things get weird in the market. The individuals who have failed to achieve market returns (see Chapter 16) are the ones who panic (selling after large declines and buying after large increases). The long-term buy-and-hold investor earns the returns of the market.

Chapter 34
Rebalancing

> Abstract - Don't rebalance too frequently – once a year is enough. The concept is simple, just try to maintain your original asset allocation percentages through time. Rebalancing will increase your return by causing you to sell high and buy low.

A Modern Portfolio Theory portfolio does not behave like the rest of the market. There will be times when you will be very far out of step with the news reports about the market (the "Dow", the NASDAQ and the S&P 500). From my experience, these are trying times. Like the period from 1995 through 1998 when the S&P 500 outperformed everything. I was underperforming the "market", with an average return across those years of around 15% when the S&P 500 averaged over 28%. But then there's the flip side, like all through 2000 and 2001. Those times were kind of fun; all the puzzled looks from friends and associates who were losing their shirts in those years and asking me **"how can you be UP in a market like this?"**. This phenomenon is called "tracking error" by academics; whatever you chose to call it, get used to it. You have intentionally included asset classes in your portfolio that are poorly correlated with the market. In the long run you will benefit; in the short run you will just have to smile.

The concept of rebalancing is simple. You just try to maintain your original asset allocation percentages through time. The idea of rebalancing may even sound benign, but you will probably have to **force** yourself to put your hard earned money into an asset class that looks like a dog (like value funds during that S&P 500 run in the late 90's). You may even question the wisdom of something so counterintuitive. But if you persevere, you will establish the discipline of buying low and selling high. Eventually it will even be fun to have such "bargains" available.

Over time you will find yourself paying less and less attention to the day-to-day noise in the market and relax. The confidence of knowing that you will do about as well as it is possible to do (without 'gambling') is very reassuring. Somewhere down the road you may even stop worrying about your investments at all. You will sleep well.

The rebalancing required in your nestegg will only take a few hours at the end of each year. Your strategies will be different before and after retirement.

In the accumulation phase:

You should add any new investment money first to funds that have done poorly. If this alone does not bring the portfolio back into its asset allocation balance, you may need to transfer some from the high performers to add to the funds with the worst returns. This discipline will cause YOU to sell high and buy low (while most others are panicking and selling low and then buying high right away by chasing the high flyers which don't usually continue up).

During retirement:

In bad years, withdraw only from fixed income (to allow the equity funds to recover).
In good years, withdraw first from the top performing equity funds, then second from all funds pro-rata to maintain allocation. (see Chapters 36 and 37)

Don't bother trying to get all the funds exactly on their allocation percentages (A good rule of thumb is to keep percentages within 5% of their targets). Don't rebalance too frequently – once a year (or even every two years) is enough. In addition to reducing return, the tax impact of overly aggressive reallocation can become significant.

Chapter 35
Investment Policy

Abstract - Most investors benefit from spelling out their investment policy in writing and in detail. The only time your investment policy should change is in response to significant life changes in your financial condition, objectives or time horizons.

Write it down; then stick to it.

An Investment Policy should include your goals, objectives and strategies for:

1. **Cash reserves** – say 6 months normal spending
2. **General goals and objectives** – regarding saving for a house, kids' college, retirement, etc. (money for very short term goals should be shifted into cash reserves)
3. **Time Horizon**
4. **Risk** (maximum loss you are willing to accept in any one year)
5. **Asset Classes** (to be in Portfolio)
    a. Fixed Income
    b. Large Cap
    c. Small Cap
    d. Value
    e. International
    f. Emerging Markets
6. **Rebalancing strategy**
7. **Withdrawal strategy** (in retirement)

The only time your investment policy should change is in response to significant life changes in your financial condition, objectives or time horizon. Otherwise, stay the course.

> *"History teaches that both investment managers and clients need help if they are to hold successfully to the discipline of long-term commitments. This means restraining themselves from reacting to disconcerting short-term data and keeping themselves from taking those unwise actions that seem so 'obvious' and urgent to optimists at market highs and pessimists at market lows. In short, policy is the most powerful antidote to panic."*

> *"For investors, the real opportunity to achieve superior results is not in scrambling to outperform the market, but in establishing and adhering to appropriate investment policies over the long term – policies that position the portfolio to benefit from riding with the main long term forces of the market."*

> Charles Ellis, The Loser's Game, p 23, 60

Part Five

Retirement

Chapter 36
Retirement Calculators and Withdrawal Strategies

> Abstract - Beware of retirement calculators – many of them overstate the amount you can safely withdraw from your nestegg in retirement. On the other hand some are so conservative that they will have you living like a pauper while your money piles up for your heirs.

Beware of overly simplistic retirement calculators. Overconfidence in high returns and low deviation from averages can cause higher withdrawals than can be supported through the market downturns we should reasonably expect. For example, just because you expect 11% returns with 3% inflation does not mean you can withdraw the 8% difference every year. Your nestegg will be decimated if the market declines by 25% or 30% for a few years, which you should expect to happen sometime during your life. If it happens in your first year of retirement, it would be very bad news. If you continued high withdrawals, your nestegg would not recover and you would run out of money!

Most reputable financial planners have abandoned the "linear" calculators that produced those high withdrawals.

I have seen retirement calculators that recommend everything from 3% of nestegg to 8% of nestegg withdrawal rates, and of course there's the old 5% rule used by bank trust departments over the years. Recently there have been a handful of careful studies that seem to argue for very small withdrawals (in the 3% to 5% range).

Perhaps most notable among these has come to be known as "the Trinity Study" published in 1997 by Phillip L. Cooley, Carl M. Hubbard and Daniel T. Walz, three faculty members of Trinity University. Their backtesting study looked at the periods from 1926 to 1995. They used the returns from a portfolio consisting of only the S&P 500 and long-term high-grade corporate bonds. They concluded that only a withdrawal rate of from 4% to 5% of the initial portfolio value (e.g. $40,000 or $50,000 from a $1,000,000 portfolio) had a reasonable expectation of success.

William Bernstein published his "Retirement Calculator from Hell" in 1998. He makes the point that even 4% or 5% can be disastrous if you retire just before the next market collapse. In his Retirement Calculator from Hell – Part II and Part III (both published in 2001) he shares more gloom. You should read all of these if you're feeling cocky about higher withdrawal rates. Stuff happens – really (you can find them at www.efficientfrontier.com).

So, how sure do you want to be? If you want to be 100% (well, let's say 99.5%) sure, you should not withdraw more than 3%. But if you limit your withdrawals that much, you will very likely leave a very big estate for the kids (and the tax man) and sacrifice more lifestyle than you need to.

One of the problems with most of these studies is that they use an S&P 500 dominated portfolio that ignores most of the advantages of Modern Portfolio Theory. Remember, the S&P 500 has had an average return of about 11% per year, but with a standard deviation of about 20% (far more volatile than a Modern Portfolio Theory portfolio).

A few years ago Nolan Jones of Optima Asset Management in Dallas, Texas, did a similar study using a lot of small cap and small cap value in the portfolios. Scott Burns published some of his data in his column on July 18, 2000 in the Dallas Morning News (available at www.scottburns.com). A mixed portfolio of "small cap and small value" was found to support a 6.7% withdrawal rate. A portfolio of only small cap value would support 10.6% withdrawals. Nolan doesn't recommend withdrawal rates over 8%, but his study provides at least some preliminary data about the performance of modern portfolios.

One of the differences between Nolan Jones' study and the others above is that he uses random future events with historical average return and standard deviation instead of a linear replication of the precise series of historical daily, monthly, and yearly returns that occurred in the past. A whole new family of software and modeling techniques have evolved in recent years around **stochastic analysis** (the study of random events). Using these techniques, it is possible to determine the chances of success in a new and more interesting way.

The analysis technique and software is called "Monte Carlo" analysis. With the Monte Carlo software I use I can determine not only that a withdrawal rate has an 85% chance of survival for 40 years, but also that it has a 50% chance of doubling my nestegg in real terms. That's the kind of balance I want. I don't want to run out of money, but I also don't want to have it pile up on me unused either.

The "**Sleep Well Withdrawal Strategies**" in the next chapter are a good middle ground.

Chapter 37
Three Sleep Well Withdrawal Strategies

> Abstract – Keep 25% in fixed income assets to provide for several years of normal expenses. This rainy day fund will allow you to sleep well. Strategies are outlined for 4%, 5% and 6% withdrawal rates.

In order to sleep well, with money in the stock market, most of us need a rainy day fund. With four, five, or maybe even six years of normal expenses in fixed income assets, most people will have a better chance of avoiding a panic reaction in one of the nasty stock market "collapses" that are sure to come. When the stock market falls, you can withdraw from your fixed income assets for a while.

All three Sleep Well Withdrawal Strategies use a 25% fixed income allocation during retirement to provide for several years of normal expenses. The basic idea is simple:

In the good stock market years withdraw from whatever did best,
(to rebalance);

In the bad stock market years withdraw from the fixed income assets
(to allow the stock funds to recover).

Strategy A – for those who are comfortable with being 85% certain they won't run out of money (and a good chance of winding up with a lot more than you started with).

Start with an initial withdrawal rate of **6% of nestegg**. And then in the next year, either increase the dollar amount by inflation (if the market is up) or take the same 6% times the new lower nestegg amount (if the market has gone down).

This system will require you to reduce expenses following bad market years, but you probably would have done so anyway – keeping at least marginally in step with emotions of the market itself. If your withdrawals become too small to live on, you have two choices: take on some part time work to make up the short fall or go back to work full time for a while. The chance of this happening is less than 15%, but it could happen.

Strategy B – for those who need to be a little more sure they won't run out of money.

Start with an initial withdrawal rate of **5% of nestegg**, and then in the following years adjust the dollar amount for inflation. This lump sum with inflation adjustment approach will probably cause your nestegg to grow quite large, but there is very little chance of running out of money.

Strategy C – for the real chickens among us who simply can't deal with uncertainty.

Reduce your initial withdrawal rate to **4% of nestegg** and then in the following years adjust the dollar amount for inflation (as in strategy B).

Chapter 38
Boomers and Social Security
Will It be there for Us?

Abstract - Social Security will probably be there for all boomers. But the benefits may be marginally lower; the Normal Retirement Age will probably increase again; and the early retirement age may be increased.

The Social Security Act of 1935 provides (some) guaranteed retirement money for all.

Social Security's reserves began accumulating in 1977. It continues today to take in more than it is paying out – the "reserve" (the excess) is being held in government bonds. The bean counters at Social Security project they will continue to be able to pay benefits solely from current revenue until 2016. From 2017 to 2026, Social Security will have to draw more heavily from the interest on their government bonds. After 2026, Social Security will need to start cashing in those bonds, which will run out in 2038. After 2038, the bean counters project that there will only be enough revenue from taxes to pay 72% of benefits.

The normal retirement age (NRA) was established by the original Social Security Act at 65; and the NRA remained 65 until it was changed in 1983. This change was partly in response to the looming demographic problem of 80 million retiring baby boomers, and partly in response to the simple fact that life expectancy had changed dramatically. At the turn of the century (1900) the average life expectancy was only 46 years. Today it is over 70 years.

In 1983, Congress increased the Normal Retirement Age for boomers from 65 to from 66 to 67, depending on when you were born. The range of Normal Retirement Age is summarized in this table.

TABLE 38.1   NORMAL RETIREMENT AGE

Year of birth	Retirement Age	
1937 or before	65	
1938	65 + 2 months	
1939	65 + 4 months	
1940	65 + 6 months	
1941	65 + 8 months	
1942	65 + 10 months	
1943 to 1954	66	*1946 (the first boomers)*
1955	66 + 2 months	
1956	66 + 4 months	
1957	66 + 6 months	
1958	66 + 8 months	
1959	66 + 10 months	
1960 or later	67	*1964 (the last boomers)*

The Baby Boomers are the large number of people born between 1946 and 1964; the peak year was 1954. The 1946 cohort will reach 66 (their NRA) in 2012; the 1964 cohort will reach age 67 (their NRA) in 2031. This group of over 80 million will overwhelm the current system.

When the reserves are exhausted, in 2038, there are choices to be made (hopefully someone is clever enough to address this issue before then).

There are numerous proposals on how to close the gap. It's anyone's guess what will eventually be done, but the following things are being discussed:

1. Increasing the current payroll tax
2. Increasing the wages subject to Social Security tax
3. Taxing Social Security benefits like pension benefits
4. Including new state and government workers
5. Additional increases to the Normal Retirement Age
6. Moving the early retirement age from 62 to 63
7. Cutting benefits
8. Investing some of the trust fund in private securities
9. Creating personal Social Security retirement accounts (privatization)

Some Social Security will be there. But benefits may be marginally lower (probably not more than 10% lower), the Normal Retirement Age will likely increase again (maybe by one year), and the early retirement age may be increased (again maybe by one year).

Whatever finally gets done, it seems likely that we will all get something, eventually.

Chapter 39
Social Security Benefits

Abstract - Social Security benefits vary significantly based on your earnings and the age you retire.

The easiest (and most accurate) way to determine the amount of your estimated benefits is to look at the "Social Security Statement" you recently started receiving each year from the Social Security Administration. If you misplaced this statement (or did not yet receive one) you can request one by calling 800-772-1213 or by writing to Social Security Administration, Office of Earnings Operations, P.O. Box 33026, Baltimore, MD 21290-3026. Additional information can also be found by visiting www.ssa.gov .

The amount you would get at your normal retirement age is your Primary Insurance Amount. To qualify for benefits you must have earned 40 work credits, generally equal to about 10 years of earnings. For people born after 1928, Social Security counts your 35 years of highest earnings after 1950 (or age 21 whichever is later) to determine your benefits. For earnings before age 60, your earnings are adjusted upward by an inflation factor for each year. Earnings after age 60 are not indexed. The average of your 35 highest yearly earnings is used to determine your benefit. The Average Indexed Monthly Earnings (AIME) is used to calculate your benefits.

The formula used has three parts, creating bend points in benefits, favoring lower income workers.

The first $561 of AIME is multiplied by **90%**;
The next $2820 of AIME (up to $3,381) is multiplied by **32%**; and
All AIME over $3,381 is multiplied by **15%**.

The following example uses three hypothetical workers all age 62 in 2001: one with average earnings; one with high earnings (160% of average); and last a worker with maximum Social Security earnings.

TABLE 39.1   PIA FOR THREE HYPOTHETICAL WORKERS

	AVERAGE (A)	HIGH (B)	MAXIMUM (C)
Current Salary	$32,000	$50,000	$84,900
Total Indexed Earnings (35 yrs)	$1,068,074	$1,638,038	$2,153,125
Average Indexed Monthly Earnings	2,543	3,900	5,126
90% of first $561	504.90	504.90	504.90
32% to $3,381	634.25	902.40	902.40
15% over $3,381	0.00	77.86	261.82
Primary Insurance Amount (PIA)	1,139.15	1,485.16	1,669.12
PIA (rounded down to 0.10)	$1,139.10	$1,485.10	$1,669.10

If you are married, your spouse will receive 50% of your amount. So your benefit, if married, is at least 150% of your personal benefit amount (possibly more if your spouse has earnings too). The survivor benefit for your spouse is 100% of your benefit amount at age 65; but only 71.5% at age 60 (100% minus 0.475% per month before age 65 that the benefit is elected).

Early Retirement (age 62)

The formula for the reduction in benefits for early retirement (age 62) is a little complicated. The benefit is reduced by 5/9 of one percent for each month before your normal retirement age (up to 36 months); and then 5/12 of one percent for each month over three years before normal retirement age.

>If you retire at 62 with a normal retirement age of 66:
>36 months @ 5/9 = 20%
>12 months @ 5/12 = 5%
>total reduction for **4 years** early therefore = **25%**

>If you retire at 62 with a normal retirement age of 67:
>36 months @ 5/9 = 20%
>24 months @ 5/12 = 10%
>total reduction for **5 years** early therefore = **30%**

If you chose to retire early and elect to receive benefits early, your benefits will be permanently reduced based on these factors.

Delayed Retirement (up to age 70)

The formula for the increase in benefits for delayed retirement is less complicated. The benefit is increased for each year worked after your normal retirement age (up to age 70) by the applicable percentage from the following table.

Year of birth	Increase in Benefits per year of delayed retirement
1924 or before	3.0%
1925, 1926	3.5%
1927, 1928	4.0%
1929, 1930	4.5%
1931, 1932	5.0%
1933, 1934	5.5%
1935, 1936	6.0%
1937, 1938	6.5%
1939, 1940	7.0%
1941, 1942	7.5%
1943 or later	8.0%

Therefore all boomers (1946-1964) will have their benefits increased by 8.0% for each year worked after their normal retirement age. Since boomers' normal retirement age ranges from 66 to 67; their maximum increase in benefits ranges from 24% (3 x 8% with NRA of 67) to 32% (4 x 8% with NRA of 66).

Very Early Retirement (before age 62)

What about retirement earlier than 62, say at 58, or 55 (or even earlier)?

The impact of retirement before the age of 62 is not discussed in "Your Social Security Statement". It is also not discussed in most retirement guide books. Very early retirement will further decrease your Social Security benefits, but depending on your earnings history the impact may be smaller than you might have expected.

The impact in your individual case depends on how much your Average Indexed Monthly Earnings (AIME) is reduced by having no earnings in the years before age 62. If you have had maximum earnings since age 21 the impact will be very small indeed. If you had many sub-maximal years the impact will be a little larger. Here's some of the math.

If you retire at age 55, you are replacing your last 7 years (probably your highest earning years) with the six years from age 21 to 27 (probably not real barn-burners for earnings). But it's not as bad as it sounds, the maximums for earnings were under $10,000 until 1974, under $20,000 until 1978. Since then they have increased dramatically to $84,900 in 2001.

In the hypothetical example above we can substitute average earnings for all three workers in the years from 21 to 27 (to reflect the fact that high or maximum earnings in those years are very rare), and zero in the years from 55 to 62 (to reflect very early retirement). The following changes in AIME and PIA result:

TABLE 39.2   PIA FOR RETIREMENT AT 55

	AVERAGE (A)	HIGH (B)	MAXIMUM (C)
Working to age 62 from above:			
Total Indexed Earnings (35 yrs)	$1,068,074	$1,638,038	$2,153,125
Average Indexed Monthly Earnings	2,543	3,900	5,126
PIA (rounded down to 0.10)	$1,139.10	$1,485.10	$1,669.10
Retiring at 55:			
Total Indexed Earnings (35 yrs)	$1,034,760	$1,475,769	$1,814,128
Average Indexed Monthly Earnings	2,464	3,514	4,319
PIA (rounded down to 0.10)	$1,113.70	$1,427.20	$1,548.00
Reduction in annual PIA from retiring at 55	$25.40	$57.90	$121.10

The reduction in PIA is far smaller than might be expected from seven zeros between 55 and 62. The real show stopper for early retirement isn't Social Security, it's health insurance – discussed in the next chapter.

Summary of Social Benefits

By applying the various formulas for delayed, early or very early retirement we can arrive at a rough estimate of Social Security benefits at 55, 62, 65 and 70 for these hypothetical workers.

TABLE 39.3   SOCIAL SECURITY BENEFITS

	AVERAGE (A)		HIGH (B)		MAXIMUM (C)	
Earnings	$32,000		$50,000		over $84,900	
Benefits per:	mo	year	mo	year	mo	year
Retire at **55**	$835	$10,020	$1,070	$12,840	$1,150	$13,800
Retire at **62**	855	10,260	1,110	13,320	1,250	15,000
Retire at **65**	1,140	13,680	1,485	17,820	1,670	20,040
Retire at **70**	1,480	17,760	2,020	24,240	2,170	26,040

Note: These numbers are very rough estimates and should not be used for detailed planning. Your date of birth, earnings history, date of retirement, and choice of when to start receiving benefits will determine your exact benefit amount. In addition, you should expect some changes in the Social Security system (none of the changes being considered will increase your benefit).

The next chapter discusses health insurance in early retirement.

Chapter 40
Health Insurance in Early Retirement
Before Medicare Eligibility

Abstract - If you retire before you are eligible for Medicare (currently age 65) you will need health insurance coverage from some other source. There are only five choices.

If you don't have health insurance, you may not be able to retire before age 65. Without insurance, a serious illness, even if you recover fully, can wipe you out financially.

If you retire before you are eligible for Medicare (currently age 65) you need health insurance coverage from some other source. There are really only five choices.

1. Continuing Employer-Sponsored health coverage (very rare and getting rarer!)
2. COBRA Coverage (maximum of 18 months)
3. Private Individual Health Insurance
4. Special Group Health Insurance (small employer or professional groups)
5. State High Risk Insurance Pool (very expensive, not in every State)

Continuing Employer-Sponsored Health Insurance

Those of you who have an early retirement option with your employer are lucky – not many of us do. And employers that have such plans are desperate to get out of them because they are so expensive. In the future this option is going to become even more rare.

If your company does offer early retirement health care insurance as a benefit, you need to confirm the eligibility, tenure, premiums, coverages and lifetime caps – they could vary significantly from your situation while still working.

COBRA coverage

If you have only a short time until you are eligible for Medicare (less than 18 months), you can elect to purchase coverage under COBRA, the Consolidated Omnibus Budget Reconciliation Act. By law you are charged 102% of the group rate. COBRA offers you additional benefits under the HIPAA (the Kennedy-Kassebaum Act – the Health Insurance Portability and Accountability Act of 1996). Several states require that insurance companies that sell individual plans must offer them to individuals that qualify under HIPAA. The premiums may be prohibitive, but the coverage is available.

Private Individual Health Insurance Coverage

If you don't have access to group coverage you may be able to buy individual health insurance – but not if you have medical problems. The premiums for individual policies are based on your age, your medical history, deductibles, co-payments and lifetime caps. Several national insurance companies offer individual health insurance in a variety of states. At least one of the following five insurance companies offers individual insurance in your state:

American Family Insurance   www.american-family.com (15 states)
Blue Cross Blue Shield   www.bcbs.com (all 50 states)
Fortis Health   www.fortishealth.com
Golden Rule Insurance   www.goldenrule.com (all states except NY)
Trustmark Insurance   www.trustmarkinsurance.com

As a rule **you cannot get individual health insurance if you are in poor health**. If you have a poor medical history, they will almost always consider you a bad risk and refuse to offer you coverage, or alternatively under certain conditions they may offer you coverage only if you sign a waiver that excludes coverage for certain pre-existing conditions.

The most important variables in individual health insurance are the following:

1. **Maximum Benefit Limit** – the lifetime maximum that the policy will pay per covered person. You want at least $2,000,000 (preferably $3,000,000, if you can find it).

2. **Coinsurance Amount** – the amount of covered expenses shared on some basis like 80/20 between the insurance company and you. You will typically pay 20% of the first $10,000 of total medical expenses after your deductible (a total co-pay of about $2,000 maximum).

3. **Deductible** – the total amount each insured person must pay for covered expenses before the insurance kicks in. Deductibles typically range from $500 to as much as $10,000.

4. **Maximum Out-of-pocket Expense in a Policy Year** – the maximum combination of coinsurance and deductible expenses (in addition to your premium) you might pay in any one year. For an **individual** the amount will be the deductible plus about $2,000 coinsurance; for a **couple** the amount will be two times the deductible plus the $2,000 coinsurance. Your maximum total expense will be your premium plus the maximum out-of-pocket expenses.

Costs for individual coverage can vary extremely widely. Carefully research a variety of alternative policies. Some policies have prescription coverage, most do not. Some exclude coverage abroad. Higher deductibles can lower rates dramatically – but still provide adequate catastrophic coverage. Representative costs for $2,000,000 maximum benefit policies in the midwest are:

TABLE 40.1   RANGE OF INDIVIDUAL HEALTH CARE INSURANCE EXPENSES
all figures are annual expenses for **one person** (in the midwest in early 2002)
(max total expense = max out-of-pocket plus premium)

	$500 Deductible	$2,500 Deductible	$10,000 Deductible
age 55 - 59	$3,500 premium $6,000 max total expense	$2,500 premium $7,000 max total expense	$1,500 premium $13,500 max total expense
age 60 - 64	$4,500 per year $7,000 max total expense	$3,000 per year $7,500 max total expense	$1,700 per year $13,700 max total expense

The office of the State Insurance Commissioner in many states offers Consumers' Guides to buying private individual insurance. You should contact your state's commissioner for any advice the office is willing to give, such as additional companies offering individual insurance.

Several states have enacted either "guaranteed issue" laws or "community rating" systems. Guaranteed issue laws require insurance companies to provide insurance to individuals regardless of their health condition. Community rating systems require insurance companies to charge everyone the same premium regardless of health condition. Some even require the same premium regardless of age as well.

The result has been dramatically higher premiums in many of these states with far fewer choices for individuals. The worst states include: Kentucky, Maine, New Jersey, New York, Vermont and Washington state. States with no "guaranteed issue" laws or "community rating" systems (and therefore more competitive insurance) include: Alabama, Alaska, Arizona, Arkansas, California, Colorado, Connecticut, Delaware, Florida, Georgia, Illinois, Kansas, Maryland, Mississippi, Missouri, Montana, Nebraska, Nevada, North Carolina, Tennessee and Texas. The remainder of the states fall in between.

Special Group Health Insurance

There are a handful of mainly professional organizations that offer group health insurance to their members. These groups are not as common or generally available as you might have been led to believe. Most of the ads you see for group insurance available to individuals is really individual health insurance. Good insurance companies have no interest in underwriting groups that solicit hard to insure individuals to masquerade as a group. The exception to this rule is in states with "guaranteed issue" laws or "community rating" systems. In these states, forming a small employer group can sidestep the onerous rules for individual coverage and allow more competitive insurance.

State High Risk Insurance Pool

Thirty states currently have high risk insurance pools that are required to provide coverage to individuals who cannot get private individual health coverage because of health problems – pre-existing medical conditions. Generally, you must have exhausted all COBRA rights and been refused private individual coverage. You must also not be eligible for Medicaid.

The cost is significantly higher than private individual insurance but is capped in most states at some percentage over the average premium for private individual coverage.

States with high risk insurance pools include:

State	Phone	State	Phone
Alabama	800 513 1384	Missouri	913 681 5515
Alaska	907 269 7900	Montana	406 444 8200
Arkansas	501 378 2979	Nebraska	402 343 3337
California	916 324 4695	New Hampshire	(program starts July 2002)
Colorado	303 863 1960	New Mexico	505 623 9378
Connecticut	800 842 0004	North Dakota	701 282 1235
Florida	850 309 1200	Oklahoma	405 741 8434
Illinois	217 782 6333	Oregon	503 373 1692
Indiana	317 614 2000	South Carolina	800 868 2500 ext 42757
Iowa	515 248 2186	Tennessee	615 741 0177
Kansas	785 296 3071	Texas	512 441 7665
Kentucky	866 405 6145	Utah	801 328 8641
Louisiana	225 926 6245	Washington	425 771 1860
Minnesota	612 593 9609	Wisconsin	608 266 2833
Mississippi	601 362 0799	Wyoming	307 777 7401

Call your State Insurance Commissioner to determine local conditions.

Even if you can only find very expensive coverage, you should probably still consider it. Most of us cannot afford to self-insure for $2,000,000 in medical expenses.

Chapter 41
Medicare, Medigap and Long Term Care Insurance

Abstract - Even if you couldn't get health insurance before then, you will have it at age 65 with Medicare. But there are 'gaps' in the coverage that can be filled with Medigap insurance. Long term care insurance is expensive but needs to be considered.

The Medicare-Medicaid bill of 1965 amended the Social Security Act and established Medicare. Starting at age 65, the federal government will pay a lot of your medical bills. Even if you couldn't get health insurance before then, you will have it age 65. It has saved a lot of seniors from having their life savings wiped out by medical bills. But Medicare doesn't pay **all** of your medical bills. There are gaps in the coverage – hence Medigap insurance. And there are a lot of complicated options. (The figures below are for 2002)

Medicare Part A

Medicare Part A is the basic **hospitalization insurance** you are automatically entitled to when you reach age 65. There is **no premium to pay – it is free**. It mainly covers inpatient hospital stays, but also covers some skilled nursing care after a hospital visit, and home health care or hospice care under some circumstances.

Medicare currently pays for the first 60 days of hospitalization in full, except for a $812 deductible (for each "benefit period'). For days 61-90, you are responsible for a co-pay $203 per day. For days 91-150 (60 lifetime reserve days you can use only once), you have a co-pay of $406 per day. After that you're on your own – that's a big gap! Make sure you fill it.

TABLE 41.1   MEDICARE PART A HOSPITALIZATION COVERAGE

	Deductible or co-pay
First 60 days of hospitalization	a $812 per period deductible
Days 61 to 90	a $203 per day co-payment
Days 91 to 150 (one time 60 day lifetime reserve)	a $406 per day co-payment
After day 150	100% (no Medicare coverage at all)

You start over (new "benefit period") after you have been out of the hospital for 60 days.

The coverage for skilled nursing care is limited to 100 days; days 1-20 are fully covered, days 21-100 require a co-pay of $101.50 per day. After that you're on your own. Medicare is not long term care insurance.

TABLE 41.2   MEDICARE PART A SKILLED NURSING CARE COVERAGE

	Deductible or co-pay
First 20 days of hospitalization	$0 (fully covered)
Days 21 to 100	a $101.50 per day co-payment
After day 100	100% (no Medicare coverage at all)

Medicare Part B

Medicare Part B covers doctor's services, lab tests, outpatient hospital services, durable medical equipment and certain other services not covered by Medicare Part A. This **optional supplementary insurance** has a **premium of $54.00** per month. There is a $100 per year deductible and a co-pay of 20%. This is a great buy.

Medicare Part A and Part B are a good foundation on which to build good medical coverage; but without additional coverage, you are still exposed to potentially ruinous medical expenses and have limited your options for obtaining the care you will want.

Medicare Part C and Medigap Insurance

Medicare Part C was created by the Balanced Budget Act of 1997. This is more or less federal Medigap coverage, but it requires you to use specific doctors, hospitals and services to have your expenses covered. Premiums vary with age and states. Most of you will choose private Medigap insurance.

Medigap insurance is private supplemental insurance meant to close the gaps in coverage left by Medicare Part A and Part B. It is complicated. So complicated (and subject to abuse) that in 1992 congress required all states to standardize Medigap plans. There are now 10 basic types of Medigap policies which are standard in all states. Because the coverage is standardized, you can shop for the best price from the highest quality company. The following table summarizes the 10 Medigap Plans:

Plans	A	B	C	D	E	F	G	H	I	J
Core Benefits										
Part A Hospital (days 61-90)	x	x	x	x	x	x	x	x	x	x
Lifetime Reserve (days 91-150)	x	x	x	x	x	x	x	x	x	x
365 Life Hospital Days	x	x	x	x	x	x	x	x	x	x
Part A & B Blood	x	x	x	x	x	x	x	x	x	x
Additional Benefits										
Part A Hospital Deductible		x	x	x	x	x	x	x	x	x
Skilled Nursing Facility Coinsurance			x	x	x	x	x	x	x	x
Foreign Travel Emergency			x	x	x	x	x	x	x	x
Part B Deductible			x			x				x
At-home Recovery				x			x		x	x
Part B Excess Doctor Charges						100%	80%		100%	100%
Preventive Care and Screening					x					x
Outpatient Prescription (basic)								x	x	
Outpatient Prescription (extended)										x

The cost of Medigap coverage varies widely from around $350 per year to over $5,000 per year depending on your age and the plan you select. You should get at least three competitive quotes for the coverage level you choose.

Long Term Care Insurance

The average **annual** cost for nursing home care can range from $40,000 to over $100,000, depending on where you live and the quality of the nursing home. The average stay is from 18 to 20 months, and stays of 36 months, 48 months and even 96 months are not uncommon. A stay of these lengths can put quite a dent in most of our nesteggs. But the cost of insuring against it is very high – some would say prohibitive. If you have more than $2,000,000 you can probably self insure. If you have less than $200,000 the insurance will probably be too expensive. In between, you have to at least consider it.

The cost and coverage limits of these policies can vary widely. They can be purchased at most any age (up to age 84). Coverage limits involve: the daily rate (maybe around $150 per day); the lifetime limit (maybe around 5 years, or $275,000); the "elimination period" (the days you pay for before the insurance takes over) can range from 30 to 365 days; an inflation adjustment (maybe 5%); and a waiver of premium (maybe after 90 days in the nursing home).

The cost of coverage like this varies widely with age. Premiums for $150/day, $275,000 lifetime limit, 90 day elimination period, with inflation protection might cost somewhere near the following in the midwest.

Age	Annual Premium
45	$1,900
50	$2,000
55	$2,200
60	$2,600
65	$3,200
70	$4,100
75	$5,800
80	$8,400
84	$12,200

This is a tough call. A little over a third of all men and women over the age of 65 spend at least some time in a nursing home. Most boomers have so far chosen to self insure against this peril – I, have, too.

Chapter 42
Retirement Lifestyles

> Abstract - Retirement means freedom to pursue your personal goals, doing only what you want to do. No matter what your financial condition allows in terms of luxury, retirement can mean living life on your own terms and at your own pace. Freedom is its own reward.

Okay, so now you've got all your bases covered – **what are you going to with all your time!**

Retirement will not be the same for everyone. Some are hoping for a life of leisure; others intend to continue working in some way or other. Some are hoping for luxury; others only for comfort; still others are willing to live very simply just to have the freedom. Some have no intention of ever retiring at all (these are typically entrepreneurs who have built their businesses and just plain love their work). Most, claim at least, that they can't wait to retire.

Retirement means freedom to pursue your personal goals, and doing only what you want to do. No matter what your financial condition allows in terms of luxury, retirement can mean living life on your own terms and at your own pace.

In terms of work retirees fall into three main categories:

Not Really Retired – Nearly Full Time Work (with some additional travel and leisure)

My father never retired. He was the patriarch in a family-owned cabinet business in the midwest. At age 83, when he passed away, he still spent at least a little time in the office nearly every day. He quite simply loved his work, and would rather spend time there than just sit around. He traveled a lot over the years and lived a good life.

Semi-Retired – Part Time Work (with lots of additional travel and leisure)

The semi-retired baby boomers will have more options than those who have gone before. Retirement is being redefined by demographic necessity. In the next several years more and more boomers will chart a new course of semi-retirement by continuing in their executive positions on a part time (or consulting agreement) basis. Businesses of all sizes are losing their 'gray-haired' experience, and are beginning to negotiate new ways of keeping them around at least part time rather than losing them altogether. This trend will be growing.

Retired – no longer working at all.

Some retire early, some retire late; but when they do retire, this group really stops working and shifts gears entirely into leisure. Once you retire completely (or nearly completely) you will be spending a lot more time at home, and you may discover that the division of labor around the house needs some rethinking. If you've never done anything around the house before, you may need to find a way to contribute.

I'm in the middle group. So far I have chosen to continue working a little, while I get my bearings in the retirement lifestyle. I opted for the six day weekend, working only about three or four days a month. I can imagine that expanding into more work (if it is enjoyable) or disappearing altogether. Time will tell. In any case, I plan to play a lot more golf and travel a lot more.

No one can be sure how their personality will respond to retirement. But the freedom to do only what you want to, at your own pace, and on your own terms is really quite liberating. Freedom is its own reward.

Do as much or as little as you want. The choice is yours.

Appendices

Appendix A

Modern Portfolio Theory

The Timeline of Risk Management Breakthroughs

900   **Arabic Numerals** brought to Spain by Arabs in the expansion of Islam. By 1100 Arabic Numerals had spread to the rest of Europe by trade in the Mediterranean and by scholars attending universities in Spain. Along with it came **Al-Jabr,** Algebra.

1654   Blaise Pascal and Pierre de Fermat with Chevalier de Mere (a gambler) developed the **theory of probability**, a foundational concept in risk management.

1690   Edmund Haley (the famous English astronomer) began work on **probability-based life expectancy tables**, a breakthrough in risk management for life insurance.

1730   Abraham de Moivre observed the structure of **normal distribution** and discovered the concept of **standard deviation**.

1830   Judge Samuel Putman rendered a decision known as the **Prudent Man Rule** which remained the standard of care for financial trustees until the tenets of Modern Portfolio Theory was incorporated in the 1992 Prudent Investor Rule, now law in many states.

1875   Francis Galton (an amateur mathematician, and Charles Darwin's cousin) discovered **regression to the mean**.

1900   Louis Bachelier developed a theory of the random character of stock prices, the foundational insight of the **Random Walk Theory** and **Efficient Market** (Bachelier's was ahead of his time and his work remained unknown until discovered in 1964 by Paul Samuelson).

1933   Alfred Cowles reviewed approximately 12,000 recommendations and four years of transactions of 20 leading companies. In 1944 he published a follow up study reviewing 6,900 market forecasts over a period of 15.5 years. In both studies Cowles concluded that there was no evidence supporting the ability of forecasters to predict the market.

1938   Alfred Cowles created a market index, today known as the **Standard & Poors 500 Index**.

1952   Harry Markowitz published **Portfolio Selection** (a paper he later expanded into his 1959 book: Portfolio Selection: **Efficient Diversification**). His theory of portfolio selection balanced expected return and risk, measured by standard deviation.

1958   Franco Modigliani and Merton Miller developed the Modigliani-Miller (MM) Theorems, **The Cost of Capital, Corporate Finance and the Theory of Investment**.

1964   William Sharpe developed the **Capital Asset Pricing Model** (CAPM), the model assigns a 'beta' of 1.0 to the market and tracks over- and underperformance of individual stocks to the market.

1965	Paul Samuelson discovered Bachelier's (1900) work in the library of the University of Paris. Samuelson published his own "Proof that Properly Anticipated Prices Fluctuate Randomly" (**the modern beginnings of the Random Walk Theory**).
1965	Eugene Fama building on the ideas of Bachelier, Cowles and Samuelson, coined the phrase "**Efficient Market**."
1965	Michael Jensen published "The Performance of Mutual Funds in the Period 1945-1965", **the first study documenting the failure of actively managed funds to outperform appropriate indexes.**
1971	John McQuown formed the **first index fund** (Wells Fargo Bank) holding an equal dollar amount of each of the 1500 stocks on the NYSE.
1973	**S&P 500 Index Funds** established at Wells Fargo Bank and American National Bank.
1975	John Bogle and the Vanguard Group offer the **first retail index fund**.
1981	Dimensional Funds Advisors (DFA) founded offering Modern Portfolio Theory index funds to institutional investors.
1990	William F. Sharpe, Merton H. Miller and Harry M. Markowitz are awarded the **Nobel Prize** in Economic Sciences for their contribution to **Modern Portfolio Theory**.
1992	Eugene Fama and Kenneth French the **Three Factor Asset Pricing Model** published in "Size and Book-to-market Equity: Returns and Economic Fundamentals" **documenting increased returns from small cap and value asset classes**.
1992	In response to overwhelming body of evidence about the unsatisfactory performance of active managers and the benefits of passive asset class investing, the American Law Institute rewrote the **Prudent Investor Rule**.

Appendix B
Reading List and Web Sites

Reading List

Frank Armstrong, **Investment Strategies for the 21st Century**, (*online www.investorsolutions.com*) 1995-97; published as The Informed Investor, AMACOM, 2002

Peter L. Bernstein, **Capital Ideas**, The Improbable Origins of Modern Wall Street, Free Press, 1992

Peter L. Bernstein, **Against The Gods**, The Remarkable Story of Risk, Wiley, 1998

William J. Bernstein, **The Intelligent Asset Allocator**, How to Build Your Portfolio to Maximize Returns and Minimize Risk, McGraw Hill, 2000

John J. Bowen and Daniel C. Goodie, **The Prudent Investor's Guide to Beating Wall Street at Its Own Game**, McGraw Hill, 1998

Charles D. Ellis, **Winning the Loser's Game**, Timeless Strategies for Successful Investing, McGraw Hill, 1998 *(revised edition of Investment Policy 1993)*

Charles D. Ellis with James R. Vertin, **The Investor's Anthology**, Original Ideas from the Industry's Greatest Minds, Wiley, 1997

Benjamin Graham, **The Intelligent Investor**, Harper & Row, 1973

Robert A. Haugen, **The New Finance: The Case Against Efficient Markets**, Prentice Hall, 1995 (a great argument for value investing)

Burton G. Malkiel, **A Random Walk Down Wall Street**, Norton, 1996, 1973

John Merrill, **Beyond Stocks, A Guide to Better Performing Complete Portfolios**, Tanglwood Publishing, 1997

Jeremy Siegel, **Stocks fo the Long Run**, McGraw Hill, 1998

Thomas J. Stanley and William D. Danko, **The Millionaire Next Door, The Surprising Secrets of America's Wealthy**, Longstreet Press, 1996

Larry E. Swedroe, **The Only Guide to a Winning Investment Strategy You'll Ever Need**, Index Funds and Beyond – The Way Smart Money Invests Today, TT Dutton, 1998

Larry E. Swedroe, **What Wall Street Doesn't Want You To Know**, How You Can Build Real Wealth Investing in Index Funds, TT Dutton, 2001

David F. Swensen, **Pioneering Portfolio Management**, An Unconventional Approach to Institutional Management, Free Press, 2000

Mitch Anthony, **The New Retire-Mentality**, Planning Your Life and Living Your Dreams at any Age *You* Want, Dearborn Trade, 2001

Gillette Edmunds, **How to Retire Early and Live Well**, with Less than a Million Dollars, Adams Media, 2000

Stan Hinden, **How to Retire Happy**, Everything You Need to Know About the 12 Most Important Decisions You Must Make Before You Retire, McGraw Hill, 2001

Web Sites

www.dfafunds.com
Dimensional Funds Advisors (DFA)
Great Modern Portfolio Theory index funds
Good information

www.vanguard.com
The Vanguard Group
Good Modern Portfolio Theory index funds
Good information

www.enansonasset.com
Evanson Asset Management
Steven Evanson
Fee-only-advisor (flat fees)
Good overview of Modern Portfolio Theory

www.efficientfrontier.com
Efficient Frontier Advisors
William J. Bernstein
Fee-only-advisor (percentage based fees)
Good, very detail oriented newsletter (Efficient Frontier)

www.investorsolutions.com
Investor Solutions Inc.
Frank Armstrong
Fee-only-advisor (percentage based fees)
Good newsletter
Great online book (Investment Strategies for the 21st Century)

www.tamasset.com
TAM Asset Management Inc.
Jeffrey C. Troutner
Fee-only-advisor (percentage based fees)
Great newsletter (Asset Class)

Appendix C
Lifestyle Overhead & Compounding

The Power of Compounding

From Chapter 2 The Power of Compounding

A Penny Doubled (every day for a month)

Day	Accrued Total
1	0.01
2	0.02
3	0.04
4	0.08
5	0.16
6	0.32
7	0.64
8	1.28
9	2.56
10	5.12
11	10.24
12	20.48
13	40.96
14	81.92
15	163.84
16	327.68
17	655.36
18	1,310.72
19	2,621.44
20	5,242.88
21	10,485.76
22	20,971.52
23	41,943.04
24	83,886.08
25	167,772.16
26	335,544.32
27	671,088.64
28	1,342,177.28
29	2,684,354.56
30	**$5,368,709.12**

The Power of Compounding
40 Year Investment Pro-Forma
Tax-Deferred

$1,000 per year

age	beg bal	deposits	10% return	0% taxes	end balance
1	0	1,000	100	0	1,100
2	1,100	1,000	210	0	2,310
3	2,310	1,000	331	0	3,641
4	3,641	1,000	464	0	5,105
5	5,105	1,000	611	0	6,716
6	6,716	1,000	772	0	8,487
7	8,487	1,000	949	0	10,436
8	10,436	1,000	1,144	0	12,579
9	12,579	1,000	1,358	0	14,937
10	14,937	1,000	1,594	0	$17,531
11	17,531	1,000	1,853	0	20,384
12	20,384	1,000	2,138	0	23,523
13	23,523	1,000	2,452	0	26,975
14	26,975	1,000	2,797	0	30,772
15	30,772	1,000	3,177	0	34,950
16	34,950	1,000	3,595	0	39,545
17	39,545	1,000	4,054	0	44,599
18	44,599	1,000	4,560	0	50,159
19	50,159	1,000	5,116	0	56,275
20	56,275	1,000	5,727	0	$63,002
21	63,002	1,000	6,400	0	70,403
22	70,403	1,000	7,140	0	78,543
23	78,543	1,000	7,954	0	87,497
24	87,497	1,000	8,850	0	97,347
25	97,347	1,000	9,835	0	108,182
26	108,182	1,000	10,918	0	120,100
27	120,100	1,000	12,110	0	133,210
28	133,210	1,000	13,421	0	147,631
29	147,631	1,000	14,863	0	163,494
30	163,494	1,000	16,449	0	$180,943
31	180,943	1,000	18,194	0	200,138
32	200,138	1,000	20,114	0	221,252
33	221,252	1,000	22,225	0	244,477
34	244,477	1,000	24,548	0	270,024
35	270,024	1,000	27,102	0	298,127
36	298,127	1,000	29,913	0	329,039
37	329,039	1,000	33,004	0	363,043
38	363,043	1,000	36,404	0	400,448
39	400,448	1,000	40,145	0	441,593
40	441,593	1,000	44,259	0	$486,852
		$40,000			

The Power of Compounding
40 Year Investment Pro-Forma
Tax-Deferred

$3,000 per year

age	beg bal	deposits	10% return	0% taxes	end balance
1	0	3,000	300	0	3,300
2	3,300	3,000	630	0	6,930
3	6,930	3,000	993	0	10,923
4	10,923	3,000	1,392	0	15,315
5	15,315	3,000	1,832	0	20,147
6	20,147	3,000	2,315	0	25,462
7	25,462	3,000	2,846	0	31,308
8	31,308	3,000	3,431	0	37,738
9	37,738	3,000	4,074	0	44,812
10	44,812	3,000	4,781	0	$52,594
11	52,594	3,000	5,559	0	61,153
12	61,153	3,000	6,415	0	70,568
13	70,568	3,000	7,357	0	80,925
14	80,925	3,000	8,392	0	92,317
15	92,317	3,000	9,532	0	104,849
16	104,849	3,000	10,785	0	118,634
17	118,634	3,000	12,163	0	133,798
18	133,798	3,000	13,680	0	150,477
19	150,477	3,000	15,348	0	168,825
20	168,825	3,000	17,182	0	$189,007
21	189,007	3,000	19,201	0	211,208
22	211,208	3,000	21,421	0	235,629
23	235,629	3,000	23,863	0	262,492
24	262,492	3,000	26,549	0	292,041
25	292,041	3,000	29,504	0	324,545
26	324,545	3,000	32,755	0	360,300
27	360,300	3,000	36,330	0	399,630
28	399,630	3,000	40,263	0	442,893
29	442,893	3,000	44,589	0	490,482
30	490,482	3,000	49,348	0	$542,830
31	542,830	3,000	54,583	0	600,413
32	600,413	3,000	60,341	0	663,755
33	663,755	3,000	66,675	0	733,430
34	733,430	3,000	73,643	0	810,073
35	810,073	3,000	81,307	0	894,380
36	894,380	3,000	89,738	0	987,118
37	987,118	3,000	99,012	0	1,089,130
38	1,089,130	3,000	109,213	0	1,201,343
39	1,201,343	3,000	120,434	0	1,324,778
40	1,324,778	3,000	132,778	0	$1,460,555
		$120,000			

The Power of Compounding
40 Year Investment Pro-Forma
Tax-Deferred

$5,000 per year

age	beg bal	deposits	10% return	0% taxes	end balance
1	0	5,000	500	0	5,500
2	5,500	5,000	1,050	0	11,550
3	11,550	5,000	1,655	0	18,205
4	18,205	5,000	2,321	0	25,526
5	25,526	5,000	3,053	0	33,578
6	33,578	5,000	3,858	0	42,436
7	42,436	5,000	4,744	0	52,179
8	52,179	5,000	5,718	0	62,897
9	62,897	5,000	6,790	0	74,687
10	74,687	5,000	7,969	0	$87,656
11	87,656	5,000	9,266	0	101,921
12	101,921	5,000	10,692	0	117,614
13	117,614	5,000	12,261	0	134,875
14	134,875	5,000	13,987	0	153,862
15	153,862	5,000	15,886	0	174,749
16	174,749	5,000	17,975	0	197,724
17	197,724	5,000	20,272	0	222,996
18	222,996	5,000	22,800	0	250,795
19	250,795	5,000	25,580	0	281,375
20	281,375	5,000	28,637	0	$315,012
21	315,012	5,000	32,001	0	352,014
22	352,014	5,000	35,701	0	392,715
23	392,715	5,000	39,772	0	437,487
24	437,487	5,000	44,249	0	486,735
25	486,735	5,000	49,174	0	540,909
26	540,909	5,000	54,591	0	600,500
27	600,500	5,000	60,550	0	666,050
28	666,050	5,000	67,105	0	738,155
29	738,155	5,000	74,315	0	817,470
30	817,470	5,000	82,247	0	$904,717
31	904,717	5,000	90,972	0	1,000,689
32	1,000,689	5,000	100,569	0	1,106,258
33	1,106,258	5,000	111,126	0	1,222,383
34	1,222,383	5,000	122,738	0	1,350,122
35	1,350,122	5,000	135,512	0	1,490,634
36	1,490,634	5,000	149,563	0	1,645,197
37	1,645,197	5,000	165,020	0	1,815,217
38	1,815,217	5,000	182,022	0	2,002,239
39	2,002,239	5,000	200,724	0	2,207,963
40	2,207,963	5,000	221,296	0	$2,434,259
		$200,000			

The Power of Compounding
40 Year Investment Pro-Forma
Tax-Deferred

$10,000 per year

age	beg bal	deposits	10% return	0% taxes	end balance
1	0	10,000	1,000	0	11,000
2	11,000	10,000	2,100	0	23,100
3	23,100	10,000	3,310	0	36,410
4	36,410	10,000	4,641	0	51,051
5	51,051	10,000	6,105	0	67,156
6	67,156	10,000	7,716	0	84,872
7	84,872	10,000	9,487	0	104,359
8	104,359	10,000	11,436	0	125,795
9	125,795	10,000	13,579	0	149,374
10	149,374	10,000	15,937	0	$175,312
11	175,312	10,000	18,531	0	203,843
12	203,843	10,000	21,384	0	235,227
13	235,227	10,000	24,523	0	269,750
14	269,750	10,000	27,975	0	307,725
15	307,725	10,000	31,772	0	349,497
16	349,497	10,000	35,950	0	395,447
17	395,447	10,000	40,545	0	445,992
18	445,992	10,000	45,599	0	501,591
19	501,591	10,000	51,159	0	562,750
20	562,750	10,000	57,275	0	$630,025
21	630,025	10,000	64,002	0	704,027
22	704,027	10,000	71,403	0	785,430
23	785,430	10,000	79,543	0	874,973
24	874,973	10,000	88,497	0	973,471
25	973,471	10,000	98,347	0	1,081,818
26	1,081,818	10,000	109,182	0	1,200,999
27	1,200,999	10,000	121,100	0	1,332,099
28	1,332,099	10,000	134,210	0	1,476,309
29	1,476,309	10,000	148,631	0	1,634,940
30	1,634,940	10,000	164,494	0	$1,809,434
31	1,809,434	10,000	181,943	0	2,001,378
32	2,001,378	10,000	201,138	0	2,212,515
33	2,212,515	10,000	222,252	0	2,444,767
34	2,444,767	10,000	245,477	0	2,700,244
35	2,700,244	10,000	271,024	0	2,981,268
36	2,981,268	10,000	299,127	0	3,290,395
37	3,290,395	10,000	330,039	0	3,630,434
38	3,630,434	10,000	364,043	0	4,004,478
39	4,004,478	10,000	401,448	0	4,415,926
40	4,415,926	10,000	442,593	0	$4,868,518
		$400,000			

The Power of Compounding
40 Year Investment Pro-Forma
Taxable (assuming 32% total state and federal taxes)

$1,000 per year

age	beg bal	deposits	10% return	**32% taxes**	end balance
1	0	1,000	100	32	1,068
2	1,068	1,000	207	66	2,209
3	2,209	1,000	321	103	3,427
4	3,427	1,000	443	142	4,728
5	4,728	1,000	573	183	6,117
6	6,117	1,000	712	228	7,601
7	7,601	1,000	860	275	9,186
8	9,186	1,000	1,019	326	10,879
9	10,879	1,000	1,188	380	12,687
10	12,687	1,000	1,369	438	$14,617
11	14,617	1,000	1,562	500	16,679
12	16,679	1,000	1,768	566	18,881
13	18,881	1,000	1,988	636	21,233
14	21,233	1,000	2,223	711	23,745
15	23,745	1,000	2,475	792	26,428
16	26,428	1,000	2,743	878	29,293
17	29,293	1,000	3,029	969	32,353
18	32,353	1,000	3,335	1,067	35,621
19	35,621	1,000	3,662	1,172	39,111
20	39,111	1,000	4,011	1,284	$42,839
21	42,839	1,000	4,384	1,403	46,820
22	46,820	1,000	4,782	1,530	51,072
23	51,072	1,000	5,207	1,666	55,612
24	55,612	1,000	5,661	1,812	60,462
25	60,462	1,000	6,146	1,967	65,642
26	65,642	1,000	6,664	2,133	71,173
27	71,173	1,000	7,217	2,310	77,081
28	77,081	1,000	7,808	2,499	83,390
29	83,390	1,000	8,439	2,700	90,129
30	90,129	1,000	9,113	2,916	$97,326
31	97,326	1,000	9,833	3,146	105,012
32	105,012	1,000	10,601	3,392	113,221
33	113,221	1,000	11,422	3,655	121,988
34	121,988	1,000	12,299	3,936	131,351
35	131,351	1,000	13,235	4,235	141,351
36	141,351	1,000	14,235	4,555	152,031
37	152,031	1,000	15,303	4,897	163,437
38	163,437	1,000	16,444	5,262	175,618
39	175,618	1,000	17,662	5,652	188,628
40	188,628	1,000	18,963	6,068	$202,523
		$40,000			

The Power of Compounding
40 Year Investment Pro-Forma
Taxable (assuming 32% total state and federal taxes)

$3,000 per year

age	beg bal	deposits	10% return	**32% taxes**	end balance
1	0	3,000	300	96	3,204
2	3,204	3,000	620	199	6,626
3	6,626	3,000	963	308	10,280
4	10,280	3,000	1,328	425	14,184
5	14,184	3,000	1,718	550	18,352
6	18,352	3,000	2,135	683	22,804
7	22,804	3,000	2,580	826	27,559
8	27,559	3,000	3,056	978	32,637
9	32,637	3,000	3,564	1,140	38,060
10	38,060	3,000	4,106	1,314	$43,852
11	43,852	3,000	4,685	1,499	50,038
12	50,038	3,000	5,304	1,697	56,644
13	56,644	3,000	5,964	1,909	63,700
14	63,700	3,000	6,670	2,134	71,236
15	71,236	3,000	7,424	2,376	79,284
16	79,284	3,000	8,228	2,633	87,879
17	87,879	3,000	9,088	2,908	97,059
18	97,059	3,000	10,006	3,202	106,863
19	106,863	3,000	10,986	3,516	117,334
20	117,334	3,000	12,033	3,851	$128,516
21	128,516	3,000	13,152	4,209	140,459
22	140,459	3,000	14,346	4,591	153,215
23	153,215	3,000	15,621	4,999	166,837
24	166,837	3,000	16,984	5,435	181,386
25	181,386	3,000	18,439	5,900	196,925
26	196,925	3,000	19,992	6,398	213,519
27	213,519	3,000	21,652	6,929	231,243
28	231,243	3,000	23,424	7,496	250,171
29	250,171	3,000	25,317	8,101	270,387
30	270,387	3,000	27,339	8,748	$291,977
31	291,977	3,000	29,498	9,439	315,036
32	315,036	3,000	31,804	10,177	339,662
33	339,662	3,000	34,266	10,965	365,963
34	365,963	3,000	36,896	11,807	394,053
35	394,053	3,000	39,705	12,706	424,052
36	424,052	3,000	42,705	13,666	456,092
37	456,092	3,000	45,909	14,691	490,310
38	490,310	3,000	49,331	15,786	526,855
39	526,855	3,000	52,986	16,955	565,885
40	565,885	3,000	56,889	18,204	$607,569
		$120,000			

The Power of Compounding
40 Year Investment Pro-Forma
Taxable (assuming 32% total state and federal taxes)

$5,000 per year

age	beg bal	deposits	10% return	**32% taxes**	end balance
1	0	5,000	500	160	5,340
2	5,340	5,000	1,034	331	11,043
3	11,043	5,000	1,604	513	17,134
4	17,134	5,000	2,213	708	23,639
5	23,639	5,000	2,864	916	30,587
6	30,587	5,000	3,559	1,139	38,007
7	38,007	5,000	4,301	1,376	45,931
8	45,931	5,000	5,093	1,630	54,394
9	54,394	5,000	5,939	1,901	63,433
10	63,433	5,000	6,843	2,190	$73,087
11	73,087	5,000	7,809	2,499	83,396
12	83,396	5,000	8,840	2,829	94,407
13	94,407	5,000	9,941	3,181	106,167
14	106,167	5,000	11,117	3,557	118,726
15	118,726	5,000	12,373	3,959	132,140
16	132,140	5,000	13,714	4,388	146,465
17	146,465	5,000	15,147	4,847	161,765
18	161,765	5,000	16,676	5,336	178,105
19	178,105	5,000	18,311	5,859	195,556
20	195,556	5,000	20,056	6,418	$214,194
21	214,194	5,000	21,919	7,014	234,099
22	234,099	5,000	23,910	7,651	255,358
23	255,358	5,000	26,036	8,331	278,062
24	278,062	5,000	28,306	9,058	302,310
25	302,310	5,000	30,731	9,834	328,208
26	328,208	5,000	33,321	10,663	355,866
27	355,866	5,000	36,087	11,548	385,405
28	385,405	5,000	39,040	12,493	416,952
29	416,952	5,000	42,195	13,502	450,645
30	450,645	5,000	45,564	14,581	$486,629
31	486,629	5,000	49,163	15,732	525,059
32	525,059	5,000	53,006	16,962	566,103
33	566,103	5,000	57,110	18,275	609,938
34	609,938	5,000	61,494	19,678	656,754
35	656,754	5,000	66,175	21,176	706,754
36	706,754	5,000	71,175	22,776	760,153
37	760,153	5,000	76,515	24,485	817,183
38	817,183	5,000	82,218	26,310	878,092
39	878,092	5,000	88,309	28,259	943,142
40	943,142	5,000	94,814	30,341	$1,012,616
		$200,000			

The Power of Compounding
40 Year Investment Pro-Forma
Taxable (assuming 32% total state and federal taxes)

$10,000 per year

age	beg bal	deposits	10% return	**32% taxes**	end balance
1	0	10,000	1,000	320	10,680
2	10,680	10,000	2,068	662	22,086
3	22,086	10,000	3,209	1,027	34,268
4	34,268	10,000	4,427	1,417	47,278
5	47,278	10,000	5,728	1,833	61,173
6	61,173	10,000	7,117	2,278	76,013
7	76,013	10,000	8,601	2,752	91,862
8	91,862	10,000	10,186	3,260	108,789
9	108,789	10,000	11,879	3,801	126,866
10	126,866	10,000	13,687	4,380	$146,173
11	146,173	10,000	15,617	4,998	166,793
12	166,793	10,000	17,679	5,657	188,815
13	188,815	10,000	19,881	6,362	212,334
14	212,334	10,000	22,233	7,115	237,453
15	237,453	10,000	24,745	7,918	264,280
16	264,280	10,000	27,428	8,777	292,931
17	292,931	10,000	30,293	9,694	323,530
18	323,530	10,000	33,353	10,673	356,210
19	356,210	10,000	36,621	11,719	391,112
20	391,112	10,000	40,111	12,836	$428,388
21	428,388	10,000	43,839	14,028	468,198
22	468,198	10,000	47,820	15,302	510,716
23	510,716	10,000	52,072	16,663	556,124
24	556,124	10,000	56,612	18,116	604,621
25	604,621	10,000	61,462	19,668	656,415
26	656,415	10,000	66,642	21,325	711,731
27	711,731	10,000	72,173	23,095	770,809
28	770,809	10,000	78,081	24,986	833,904
29	833,904	10,000	84,390	27,005	901,290
30	901,290	10,000	91,129	29,161	$973,257
31	973,257	10,000	98,326	31,464	1,050,119
32	1,050,119	10,000	106,012	33,924	1,132,207
33	1,132,207	10,000	114,221	36,551	1,219,877
34	1,219,877	10,000	122,988	39,356	1,313,509
35	1,313,509	10,000	132,351	42,352	1,413,507
36	1,413,507	10,000	142,351	45,552	1,520,306
37	1,520,306	10,000	153,031	48,970	1,634,366
38	1,634,366	10,000	164,437	52,620	1,756,183
39	1,756,183	10,000	176,618	56,518	1,886,284
40	1,886,284	10,000	189,628	60,681	$2,025,231
		$400,000			

Lifestyle Overhead

From Chapter 7 Lifestyle Overhead

The $95,000 pizza and the $725,000 car

	Pizza		Car	

Assuming 10% return on investment

Age	Pizza		Car	
20	120.00	twelve ($10) pizzas		
21	252.00	every year from age 20		
22	397.20			
23	556.92			
24	732.61			
25	925.87			
26	1,138.46			
27	1,372.31			a $10,000 more expensive car
28	1,629.54			every 5 years from age 30
29	1,912.49			
30	2,223.74		10,000	new car
31	2,566.11		11,000	
32	2,942.73		12,100	
33	3,357.00		13,310	
34	3,812.70		14,641	
35	4,313.97		26,105	new car
36	4,865.36		28,716	
37	5,471.90		31,587	
38	6,139.09		34,746	
39	6,873.00		38,220	
40	7,680.30		52,043	new car
41	8,568.33		57,247	
42	9,545.16		62,971	
43	10,619.68		69,269	
44	11,801.65		76,195	
45	13,101.81		93,815	new car
46	14,531.99		103,197	
47	16,105.19		113,516	
48	17,835.71		124,868	
49	19,739.28		137,355	
50	21,833.21		161,090	new car
51	24,136.53		177,199	
52	26,670.19		194,919	
53	29,457.20		214,411	
54	32,522.92		235,852	
55	35,895.22		269,437	new car
56	39,604.74		296,381	
57	43,685.21		326,019	
58	48,173.73		358,621	
59	53,111.11		394,483	
60	58,542.22		443,931	new car
61	64,516.44		488,324	
62	71,088.08		537,157	
63	78,316.89		590,872	
64	86,268.58		649,960	
65	**$95,015.44**		**$724,955**	new car

Appendix D
Glossary

Active Management: The strategies of stock picking, trading and market timing based on various kinds of research and information in an attempt to achieve higher returns than the market or market segment.

Alpha: A measurement of a manager's or fund's risk adjusted performance based on a benchmark reflecting the fund's exposure to the market or a particular market segment. The market or market segment has, by definition, an alpha of zero. *A negative alpha is underperformance. A positive alpha is good performance.*

AMEX: The American Stock Exchange

Asset Allocation: The process of dividing one's portfolio up among various assets or asset classes. Fixed income assets and equities are generally considered the two broadest primary asset classes. Decisions regarding the amounts of value, small cap, international, emerging markets, etc. typically follow.

Asset Classes: Categories of stocks (equities), bonds and other financial assets.

Asset Class Index Funds: Index funds based on an asset class or group of asset classes.

Baby Boomer: An American born between 1946 and 1964.

Bear Market: A period of time when the price of stocks drops persistently.

Bid-Ask-Spread: The difference between the asking price (the price at which a stock is bought by a broker for an investor) and the bid price (at which it is sold by a broker to an investor). *This spread is the fee charged by the market makers – it is their overhead and profit; the cost of liquidity in our markets. The bid-ask-spread varies widely from large cap to small cap stocks and international or emerging markets. See Chapter 13.*

Book Value: An accounting term equal to a company's total assets minus its liabilities.

Book-to-Market Value: The ratio of the book value per share to the market price per share, total book value divided by market capitalization. *Stocks with high book-to-market values are considered value stocks. Stocks with low low-to-market values are growth stocks. See Chapter 24.*

Bull Market: A period of time when the price of stocks rises persistently.

Buy-and-Hold: An investment strategy that involves buying assets and holding them over the long term and selling only for rebalancing or other long term strategic reasons.

Cap: See Market Capitalization.

Commission: A fee paid to a broker to execute a trade.

Compound Interest: Interest paid on both the original investment and accumulated interest.

Compound Growth Rate (or compound rate of return): The rate at which an investment would grow (from compound interest) if the return each year was consistent rather than variable. *Return variability (volatility) reduces compound growth rate (the actual growth of each $1.00 invested).*

Correlation: The statistical measure of how strongly related two variables are. *If two assets move in exact tandem, they have a correlation of +1; if they move in exactly opposite manner, their correlation is –1.*

CRSP: Center for Research in Security Pricing.

Decile: a sub-group including 10% of the whole group.

Diversification: Allocating assets among investments with different risks, returns, and correlations in order to manage risk.

Dividend: The distribution of earnings to company shareholders, usually four times a year.

Earnings: The net earnings of a company after all expenses.

Efficient Market: The concept that all available information is rapidly digested by the market and reflected in the market prices of securities. *Stocks with high expectations have high prices; those with low expectations have low prices. In order to make money on a stock, the company must do better than everyone else is expecting (not just do well). In an efficient market, research and analysis of publicly available information will not produce excess returns.*

Emerging Markets: The capital markets of less developed countries, such as Argentina, Brazil, Chile, Greece, Hungary, Indonesia, Israel, Malaysia, Mexico, Philippines, Poland South Korea, Thailand, Turkey and others.

Equities: Stocks, real estate or other assets that an investor owns (as opposed to fixed income assets – where an investor, in effect, lends money).

Expense Ratio: The operating expenses of a mutual fund expressed as a percentage of total assets. *These expenses reflect the costs of management, research, overhead costs and certain fees. These operating expenses reduce net return. The expenses ratio does not include trading costs, which also reduce return.*

Fixed Income: Bonds, Treasury Bills, Money Market accounts etc. where an investor, in effect, lends money (as opposed to equities – where an investor owns assets).

Fundamental Analysis: The analysis of publicly available information, such as balance sheets, income statement and projections, and other indicators, in the attempt to discover "undervalued" securities.

Global Fund: A mutual fund that invests in both U.S. and international holdings. *An International Fund invests only in non-U.S. holdings.*

Growth Stock: A stock trading at a high price-to-earnings ratio (or low book-to-market value). *The market has high expectations for the growth of its earnings into the future.*

Impact Costs (or market impact costs): The increase or decrease in price caused by buying or selling a large amount of a security.

Index: A statistical model of an investment market (or market segment). *The most widely followed indexes include: The Dow Jones Industrials (the DOW); the Standard & Poor's 500 Index (the S&P 500); the NASDAQ Composite Index; the Russell 2000 (a small cap index); the Morgan Stanley EAFE Index (an international index); and the Lehman Bros Bond Index.*

Index Fund: A mutual fund that attempts to replicate the performance of a particular index, *such as the S&P 500 index, the Russell 2000 index or the EAFE index. Numerous other index funds track all manner of important market segments such as small cap, micro cap, value, international and emerging markets.*

Institutional Investors: Pension funds, banks, mutual funds, insurance companies or other large investment organizations. *Institutional investors are responsible for over 90% of trading activity in the market and therefore dominate the markets.*

International Fund: A mutual fund that invests only in non-U.S., international holdings. *A Global Fund invests in both U.S. and International holdings.*

Investment Policy: The stated (especially written) goals, objectives and strategies of an investor.

Large Cap: See Market Capitalization.

Lifestyle Overhead: The ongoing expense of the luxuries (in excess of basic necessities) we consume today at the cost of reduced savings.

Load: The commission charge that buyers of certain mutual funds must pay. The load is divided between the stockbroker, the distributor and the fund itself. Loads vary widely from around 1% to over 8%. No-load funds sell directly to investors without this commission. Loads may be front-end (paid upon purchase) or back-end, sometimes called deferred loads or fees (paid upon sale).

Market Capitalization (or market cap)**:** The market value of all of a company's stock. *Companies are frequently divided into large-cap, mid-cap, small-cap and micro-cap categories. CRSP divides market cap into deciles based on the NYSE market caps. Most stock indexes are cap-weighted, meaning that the stocks in that index are represented in proportion to their individual market capitalization. This means that such indexes are dominated by their largest growth companies.*

Market Impact Costs: Same as Impact Costs, see above.

Market Timing: Attempting to buy near the end of a bear market, or sell near the end of a bull market; or otherwise "time" trading to benefit from expected moves in the market.

Mean Variance Optimization: The mathematical technique developed by Harry Markowitz for analyzing portfolios to maximize return and minimize risk.

Mean Average (also, Mean or Average)**:** The average of a range of values *(not the median)*.

Median: The statistical center of a range of values that has the same number of values above and below it *(not the average)*.

Micro Cap: See Market Capitalization.

Modern Portfolio Theory: Risk management and asset allocation (diversification) based on the analysis of alternative portfolios composed of assets with superior interaction based on returns, risk and correlation.

Mutual Fund: An Investment Company that invests the pooled funds of individual investors in securities. Mutual funds may be either "load" funds or "no-load" funds.

NASDAQ: National Association of Securities Dealers Automated Quotations (the "over-the-counter market").

Nestegg (or personal retirement nestegg)**:** Your personal retirement savings – generally equal to your total net worth less housing, automobiles and other assets that will not be liquidated for retirement income.

Net Asset Value (NAV)**:** Price per share of a mutual fund (net assets divided by total shares outstanding).

Net Worth: Your total assets less all debt.

Nominal Return: Actual return, not adjusted for inflation.

Normal Distribution (bell curve)**:** The familiar bell-shaped curve; *A graph of frequency distribution with an equal number of events above and below average, and symmetrically distributed.*

NYSE: The New York Stock Exchange.

Passive Management: A buy-and-hold strategy rejecting the active management strategies of stock picking, trading and market timing. Asset allocation to asset classes (as a whole) or asset class index funds.

Portfolio: The various securities or mutual funds held by an investor.

Price-earnings ratio: A company's market capitalization divided by its earnings. *The p/e ratio is an indication of expectations for future earnings. The higher the p/e, the more the market is willing to pay for a company's expected earning power. A lower p/e reflects low expectations for future earnings.*

Quintile: A subgroup including 20% (1/5) of the whole group.

Rebalancing: The process of maintaining proportional portfolio asset allocations over time.

Random Walk: The theory that future stock prices are unpredictable.

Real Return: The actual nominal return adjusted for inflation. *The return of a security in excess of inflation.*

Regression to the mean: A technical term of probability and statistics. It means that, left to themselves, things tend to return to normal. *Returns, over time, tend to be subject to regression to the mean; that is, periods of over-performance tend to be followed by periods of under-performance, and vice-versa. Average returns for asset classes tend to remain stable over long periods of time.*

REIT: A Real Estate Investment Trust – an investment company that invests only in real estate.

Return: The profit from an investment.

Small Cap: See Market Capitalization.

Standard Deviation: A statistical measure of variation from average in a series of numbers, such as returns of investments). The standard deviation of returns for a security or a portfolio is usually a good estimate of its risk. Returns will be within one standard deviation of average about 68% of the time (7 out of 10 years); within two standard deviations of average about 95% of the time (19 out of 20 years); and within three standard deviations of average over 99% of the time (about 199 out of 200 years).

Total Return: Nominal return, not adjusted for inflation.

Tracking Error: The extent to which a portfolio does not directly track the market as a whole or a particular index.

Trading Costs: The total costs of commissions, bid-ask-spread, and impact costs from turnover in a mutual fund or any trading activity. *Trading costs are not included in a mutual funds expense ratio.*

Turnover: The trading activity of a mutual fund. The portion of a portfolio that is traded in a given period of time, usually expressed as a percentage per year.

Value Stock: A stock trading at a low price-to-earnings ratio (or high book-to-market value). *The market has low expectations for its earnings into the future.*

Wilshire 5000 Index: An index including all stocks traded on the NYSE, AMEX and NASDAQ. The Wilshire 5000 is a very broad index including over 6000 stocks.